WEAPON

US COMBAT SHOTGUNS

LEROY THOMPSON

Series Editor Martin Pegler

First published in Great Britain in 2013 by Osprey Publishing,
Midland House, West Way, Botley, Oxford, OX2 0PH, UK
43-01 21st Street, Suite 220B, Long Island City, NY 11101
E-mail: info@ospreypublishing.com

Osprey Publishing is part of the Osprey Group

A CIP catalog record for this book is available from the British
Library

Print ISBN: 978 1 78096 014 2
PDF ebook ISBN: 978 1 78096 016 6
ePub ebook ISBN: 978 1 78096 015 9

Index by Fionbar Lyons
Typeset in Sabon and Univers
Battlescenes by Peter Dennis
Cutaway by Alan Gilliland
Originated by PDQ Media, Bungay, UK
Printed in China through Worldprint Ltd

13 14 15 16 17 10 9 8 7 6 5 4 3 2 1

Osprey Publishing is supporting the Woodland Trust, the UK's
leading woodland conservation charity, by funding the dedication
of trees.

www.ospreypublishing.com

Acknowledgments
The author would like to thank the following for assistance in
preparing this book: Martin Floyd, Gina McNeely, John Miller,
Jeff Moeller, T. J. Mullin, Mike Spradlin, National Archives and
Records Administration, National Firearms Museum, Rock
Island Auction Service, Springfield National Historic Site.

Editor's note
For ease of comparison please refer to the following conversion
table:
1 mile = 1.6km
1yd = 0.9m
1ft = 0.3m
1in = 2.54cm/25.4mm
1lb = 0.45kg

Artist's note
Readers may care to note that the original paintings from which
the battlescenes of this book were prepared are available for
private sale. All reproduction copyright whatsoever is retained by
the Publishers. All inquiries should be addressed to:

Peter Dennis, 'Fieldhead', The Park, Mansfield, Nottinghamshire
NG18 2AT, UK, or email magie.h@ntlworld.com

The Publishers regret that they can enter into no correspondence
upon this matter.

Cover images are courtesy Rock Island Auction Company (top)
and Tom Laemlein (bottom).

CONTENTS

INTRODUCTION

Few close-combat weapons are as devastating as the combat shotgun. Though shotguns have seen at least some military service for centuries, they have been most widely used by US troops. Among the early colonists to America, the muzzle-loading blunderbuss, which often had a flared muzzle to speed loading of shot or various other metal objects, was a popular weapon that could be used for hunting as well as defense. It proved a mainstay among members of local militias and proved quite effective against Indian attacks. Crews of vessels bound to or from the New World often used the blunderbuss to repel hostile boarders, or when boarding themselves. Later, during the American Revolutionary Wars, fowling pieces were used by colonists who did not have muskets for specialized purposes such as knocking down British cavalry horses. However, the colonists might also face shotguns or blunderbusses. For example, at least one British Light Dragoon regiment raised by General John Burgoyne in 1781 was armed with blunderbusses. Muskets could also be loaded with larger shot for use at close range; General George Washington encouraged his men to load their muskets with "buck and ball" to increase hit probability.[1] In fact, some theorize that the famous admonition not to fire until "you see the whites of their eyes" was designed to maximize the effect of the buck and ball loads against the massed formations of the redcoats.

Shotguns helped defend the Alamo and were again used by US troops during the Mexican–American War of 1846–48. As the double-barreled percussion shotgun came into widespread use during the mid-19th century the scattergun's effectiveness as a combat weapon was enhanced, but it was in the hands of Confederate cavalrymen that the short double-barreled shotgun proved an especially formidable combat weapon.

1 "Buck and ball" refers to paper cartridges for muzzle-loading weapons that placed buckshot in front of a ball, thus increasing the hit probability from a muzzle-loading weapon at ranges under 200yd.

Civil War troops armed with muskets and shotguns. (Library of Congress)

Reportedly, Confederate cavalrymen often fired their shotguns at close range to blast a hole in lines of Union infantrymen. After the Civil War, the shotgun still saw usage among US troops, often for hunting game but also for guarding prisoners and protecting payrolls or other assets. During the fighting against various Indian tribes, the shotgun proved a formidable close-range weapon against the Indian horsemen. Famed Indian fighter Major General George Crook carried a double-barreled shotgun, as did other Civil War veterans under his command.

It was towards the end of the 19th century, however, that the weapon that would really be the forerunner for US 20th-century combat shotguns was developed – the Winchester Model 1897 (M97) 12-gauge pump-action shotgun. Early in its production, a short-barreled "riot gun" version of the M97 was developed. It was soon in action in the Philippines against Moro *Juramentados* ("oath-takers"). While other weapons, even the .30-caliber Krag rifle, might not stop a fanatical attacker, the M97 Riot Gun loaded with buckshot generally did.

It was as the M97 Trench Gun, however, that the Winchester achieved iconic status. Reportedly, General John Pershing was a major supporter of the issuance of shotguns to US troops during World War I, possibly because of his memories of their effectiveness during the Philippine Insurrection. As the name implies, the trench gun was developed for the trench fighting in World War I. Known to US infantrymen as the "trench broom" or "trench sweeper," the M97 Trench Gun performed that function admirably. Troops could clear a German assault on a trench by quickly pumping the shotgun and sending buckshot pellets the length of the trench. Doughboys and Marines found the trench shotgun very

effective when clearing German positions as well, especially when the enemy was inside dugouts or buildings. The major criticism was not of the M97 Trench Gun but of its ammunition, which used paper shell-casings that did not hold up in the trenches. Late in the war the availability of 12-gauge buckshot rounds loaded into brass cases alleviated the ammunition problems. A relatively small number of other combat shotguns were issued in World War I, including the Remington Model 10 (M10), Winchester Model 1912 (M12), and Remington Model 11 (M11).

After World War I, the trench shotguns and riot guns remained in service during the 1920s and 1930s where they saw service with the US Marines during the counterinsurgency "Banana Wars,"[2] and were also used when US troops were assigned to guard the US Mail and for guarding prisoners at military stockades. Labor unrest after World War I and continuing during the Great Depression also increased interest among Ordnance officers in stockpiling shotguns for use by Federal troops or members of the National Guard against "rioters."

Among the early incentives for the United States to begin acquiring more shotguns prior to entrance into World War II was the fear of parachute attacks on US air bases, or of saboteurs attacking naval bases, air bases, or other defense installations. As a result, new orders were placed for trench or riot shotguns as well as shotguns for training aerial and naval antiaircraft gunners in leading a target (in order to compensate, when shooting, for the target's movement). Initial orders were given to Winchester, Ithaca and Remington, and were increased dramatically after the attack on Pearl Harbor. Later, shotguns would also be acquired from Savage and Stevens as well.

The US Marines found the shotgun especially valuable during the jungle fighting in the Pacific. They considered it second only to the belt-fed machine gun in stopping massed Japanese attacks. Although both trench and riot shotguns were available, the Marines preferred the trench guns

---

2   The "Banana Wars" were fought in Central America and the Caribbean in defense of US economic interests.

February 2009: a trainee at the USMC Dynamic Entry School at Quantico, Virginia, practices breaching locks using a Mossberg M590 shotgun with pistol grip. (USMC)

with bayonets mounted, particularly the Winchester M97 and M12 models. According to Bruce N. Canfield, US Marines managed to acquire three times their authorized number of fighting shotguns in anticipation of the invasion of the Japanese Home Islands (Canfield 2007: 103–04). Once again, however, damp conditions caused problems with paper-cased shotgun shells. And, once again, brass shells were developed but did not reach front-line troops until very late in World War II.

The Marines had often used shotguns in conjunction with machine guns to protect the gun crews. Shotguns were again used for this mission in Korea where they also proved effective at close quarters against Chinese infiltrators or human-wave attacks. Shotguns were also used to defend command posts and supply dumps in Korea. As with other infantry weapons used during the Korean War, the shotguns were those that had been used during World War II.

In Vietnam, US troops once again found themselves involved in a jungle war where the shotgun was a highly effective weapon. The Marines made good use of the M12 Trench Guns they had deployed for decades. Even the venerable M97 Trench Gun saw use in Vietnam. Additional shotguns were acquired from other manufacturers. A substantial number of the Ithaca Model 37 (M97) Riot Gun and a few trench guns were used in Vietnam. The US Navy SEALs (Sea, Air, and Land Teams) deployed the M37, in a few cases with a "duck-bill" choke designed to spread the shot horizontally across a trail. (Actually, the "duck-bill" had been developed for the USAF Security Police in the mid-1960s in an attempt to increase hit probability for personnel guarding aircraft assigned to the Strategic Air Command and other sensitive installations.) A substantial number of Stevens Model 77E (M77E) Riot Guns were also issued in Vietnam.

The Remington Model 870 (M870) Riot Gun, the classic US police shotgun, was also acquired for military issue. Winchester's Model 1200 (M1200) Trench Gun was developed during the Vietnam War, but it saw most of its usage later. To allow the shotgun to cut an even wider swath among soldiers of the Viet Cong (VC) or North Vietnamese Army (NVA), attempts were made during the Vietnam War to increase the lethality of the fighting shotgun. One result was the Remington Model 7188 (M7188) full-automatic shotgun. Another attempt to increase lethality was the use of shotgun rounds loaded with flechettes (pointed steel projectiles).

After Vietnam, the US Department of Defense showed substantial interest in a new weapons system – the CAWS (Close Assault Weapons System) – that would fire multiple projectile rounds from a detachable box magazine in full or semiautomatic mode. Though various designs were tested, the US armed forces continued to be armed with slide-action shotguns similar to those used in World War I, primarily the Remington M870 and Winchester M1200. Beginning at the end of the 1970s, O. F. Mossberg & Sons, Inc began receiving military contracts for their Model 500 (M500) slide-action riot shotgun. Extensive competitive testing later resulted in the adoption of the military M500 by all branches of the US armed forces. A relatively small number of Mossberg Model 590 (M590) Trench Guns were also adopted by the US Marine Corps (USMC). Eventually, the M590 Riot Gun superseded the M500.

The United States had used semiautomatic riot guns, such as the Remington M11 and the Savage Model 720 (M720), during World War II, but these were emergency-issue weapons. In early 1999, however, a contract was issued for a new standard US Joint Service Combat Shotgun based on the Benelli M4 semiautomatic. Designated the Model 1014 (M1014), the new shotgun was initially ordered by the USMC. The US Navy SEALs also use the M1014. For the Army, however, the Mossberg M590 remains the primary shotgun.

In Afghanistan and, especially, Iraq, the shotgun has been used primarily for blasting the locks or hinges off doors during entries. As a result, Mossberg M590s and Remington M870s, with pistol grips to allow them to readily be carried as a supplement to the M4 carbine, have been adopted. In some cases, the breaching man was also an M249 Squad Automatic Weapon (SAW) gunner. Military police (MPs) or other troops assigned to convoy security often used shotguns as well. However, the Army has been investigating another solution for some troops needing a door-busting shotgun and a carbine. This is the Lightweight Shotgun System (LSS), which comprises a shotgun that can be mounted below the barrel of the M4 or M16, much as an M203 grenade launcher can be mounted.

Over a century after US troops employed the shotgun to stop Moros in the Philippines, US troops today deploy the shotgun in Iraq and Afghanistan against a new breed of fanatical terrorist. Development of combat shotguns for the US armed forces continues with some innovative designs such as the SRM1216, which offers large magazine capacity in a compact shotgun. US troops engaged against dangerous and determined enemies have traditionally chosen the shotgun for sure close-range stopping power. That preference for the shotgun is unlikely to change.

DEVELOPMENT
The story of the military shotgun

ORIGINS

Development of the fighting shotgun can be traced back centuries to the blunderbuss, the fowling piece, and the smoothbore musket when loaded with multiple projectiles. In the United States, the fighting shotgun developed at least partially as a matter of economics. Settlers might own a shotgun and use it primarily to kill game for food, but also employ it against Indians or other enemies. Originally, double-barreled percussion shotguns and later double-barreled cartridge shotguns proved formidable close-range weapons in the hands of cavalrymen and Western lawmen and desperadoes. It was the development of single-barreled repeating shotguns, however, that marked the beginnings of the modern US military fighting shotgun. These earliest repeating shotguns – the Winchester Model 1887 (M87) lever-action, the Winchester Model 1893 (M93) and Model 1897 (M97) slide-action weapons – first saw extensive use against train, stagecoach, and bank robbers in the American West. Although other shotguns had been used by US troops throughout the 19th century, it was the Philippine Insurrection (1899–1902) and the need for a fast-firing shotgun to stop the Moros that really initiated the military combat shotgun as it is known today.

The slide-action shotgun traditionally employs a tubular magazine and a manually operated pump forearm, which is used to chamber live rounds and extract spent rounds. It requires the forearm to be brought to the rear then pushed forward until the bolt locks to chamber or eject a cartridge, while with a semiautomatic shotgun the bolt is operated automatically by escaping gases or, with some designs, by recoil. Although the slide-action shotgun was perfected in the United States, the action itself was actually a European invention, though used for rifles. Various patents were issued

The Burgess Folding Police Shotgun, predecessor to later military and police fighting shotguns. Unlike later pump-action shotguns that used a sliding forearm, the Burgess used a sliding pistol grip to operate the action. (National Firearms Museum, NRAmuseum.org)

related to pump-action rifles during the 1850s though 1880s, primarily in Great Britain but also in France. It was Christopher Spencer, best known for the Civil War-era Spencer Repeating Rifle, who joined with Sylvester Roper to design a slide-action repeating shotgun, which was patented in April 1882. Spencer formed the Spencer Arms Company and in 1883 offered the first slide-action shotgun for sale. These early Spencer shotguns used a five-shot tubular magazine and were hammerless. However, the Spencer was more expensive than the double-barreled shotgun. As a result, only about 20,000 had been assembled prior to 1892, when production ceased.

Spencer shotguns had been intended as hunting arms, though a few were used at prisons or elsewhere in a combat role. The first slide-action shotgun marketed as a combat weapon, however, was Andrew Burgess's folding riot gun. Burgess had been involved in firearms design for many years, but it was not until 1892 that he formed the Burgess Gun Company in Buffalo, New York. Because of a Roper patent, Burgess could not use the sliding forearm mechanism of the Spencer. Instead, he was forced to use a sliding pistol grip and trigger-guard assembly. Burgess made both sporting and riot shotguns, but he is best remembered for the take-down riot model designated the "Police Gun."

Charlie Dammon, an exhibition shooter employed by the Burgess Company, helped market the shotgun by visiting Theodore Roosevelt, then President of the New York City Police Board, in 1885 (Swearengen 1978: 197). Apparently unarmed, he whipped open his coat, drew a Burgess Police Gun from the holster designed to carry it, rapidly unfolded it and locked it closed, then proceeded to fire six shots with 12-gauge blanks. Roosevelt, always interested in new firearms developments, arranged the purchase of 100 of the Burgess shotguns for the New York Penal System. Although Burgess had developed the folding riot gun for police usage, he also foresaw a market for it among cavalrymen. In spite of its innovative design, the Burgess never sold in large quantities, and in 1899 Winchester purchased the assets of the Burgess Company.

Winchester's first slide-action shotgun was the M93, designed by John Browning. Browning had also designed the Model 1890 slide-action .22 rifle, which had been highly successful, thus influencing the decision to introduce a shotgun. The M93 was a slide-action shotgun with a tubular magazine, exposed hammer, and side ejection. There were three key moving parts in operating the M93 – the bolt, the cam-operated lifter (which positioned the shell for loading and locked or unlocked the bolt), and the sliding forearm, which incorporated the action bar. Users considered the M93 superior to the Spencer because of its faster action.

SLIDE-ACTION SHOTGUNS FROM THE PHILIPPINES TO WORLD WAR II

Winchester M97

Although the M93 was quite successful, it was only produced for four years as Winchester introduced the M97 slide-action shotgun in 1897. Among the improvements over the M93 was a lengthened and strengthened receiver to take the new 2.75in smokeless-powder 12-gauge shell. An articulated shell guide was also added to prevent a shell from falling out of the ejection port before it could be chambered, a problem with the M93. A very important improvement was the addition of a slide lock, which prevented the bolt from unlocking before pressures from a fired shell had dropped. To unlock the bolt without firing the M97, it was necessary to push slightly forward on the forearm. Users of the M97 soon found this operation second nature if it were necessary to clear the action and eject a shell. A feature from the M93 retained by the M97 was the lack of firing-pin disconnect, thus allowing the trigger to be held back so the shotgun could be fired by just operating the slide action.

In 1898, the M97 Riot Gun was introduced, thus beginning the combat history of one of the most famous fighting shotguns of all times. Two versions were available – a solid-frame version with 20in barrel, and a takedown version with 21in barrel. The M97 Riot Gun achieved immediate acceptance with law officers, express guards, bank guards, railroad detectives, Texas Rangers, and others who faced dangerous criminals.

The effectiveness of the M97 Riot Gun attracted the attention of the US Ordnance Department early in the 20th century when the .38 revolvers and Krag rifles on issue in the Philippines were proving insufficient to stop frenzied Moro attackers. As a result, M97 riot guns were purchased for the Philippine Scouts and Philippine Constabulary. Units of the US Army operating along the Mexican Border acquired M97 Riot Guns as well.

Already proven in military service, the M97 was the logical choice when the United States needed a shotgun for trench clearing in World War I. General John Pershing, commander of the American Expeditionary Forces, had seen the M97 in use during the Philippine Insurrection and along the Mexican Border and was an enthusiastic advocate for equipping US troops with the fighting shotgun. When the United States entered World War I, Winchester had already been producing the M97 for 20 years and was ready to increase production to meet wartime demands.

The Winchester M97 Trench Gun with M1917 Enfield bayonet. To militarize the M97 Riot Gun, sling-swivels, a bayonet lug, and a ventilated handguard were added. (National Firearms Museum, NRAmuseum.org)

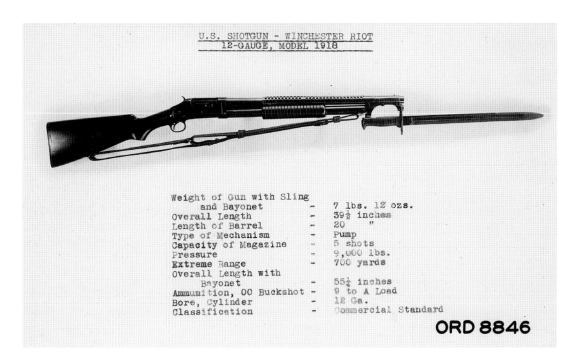

U.S. SHOTGUN - WINCHESTER RIOT
12-GAUGE, MODEL 1918

Weight of Gun with Sling and Bayonet	-	7 lbs. 12 ozs.
Overall Length	-	39½ inches
Length of Barrel	-	20 "
Type of Mechanism	-	Pump
Capacity of Magazine	-	5 shots
Pressure	-	9,000 lbs.
Extreme Range	-	700 yards
Overall Length with Bayonet	-	55¼ inches
Ammunition, 00 Buckshot	-	9 to A Load
Bore, Cylinder	-	12 Ga.
Classification	-	Commercial Standard

ORD 8846

An official Ordnance Department photograph of the M97 Trench Gun; note the designation "Model 1918 Riot Shotgun," a form of words rarely used when referring to the weapon today. (NARA)

The M97 would require some alteration, however, to meet Ordnance Department requirements, which included the addition of sling-swivels and a bayonet mount. To what would come to be known as the M97 Trench Gun, a ventilated handguard, which incorporated a front sling-swivel and a bayonet mount, was added. The rear sling-swivel was inlet into the stock. The ventilated handguard was necessary to dissipate heat when the shotgun was fired rapidly so that it could still be grasped when using the bayonet. This bayonet mount was designed to take the Model 1917 (M1917) bayonet, which was in mass production along with the M1917 rifle.

Although the term "trench gun" was normally used to describe this shotgun, the official designation was "Winchester Riot Gun, Model 1897." For the rest of this book, the term "trench gun" will be used when describing military shotguns equipped with the ventilated handguard and bayonet mount, and "riot gun" will be used for those short-barreled shotguns not equipped with the handguard and bayonet mount. To make matters more confusing, the War Department acquired some M97 "Riot Guns" during World War I which were not equipped with the handguard/bayonet mount.

World War I M97 military shotguns were 12-gauge cylinder bore, which in simple terms means that no choke device was used. The pellets exited through the full .730 hole at the end of the barrel to give a wider pattern. Determining the exact number of M97 Trench and Riot Guns delivered to the US armed forces in World War I is somewhat difficult, especially as some longer-barreled training shotguns were also acquired from Winchester. Figures supplied by Bruce Canfield would indicate a figure somewhere between 19,000 and 25,000 (Canfield 2007: 45).

Between the wars, some military trench and riot guns had been sold off to law-enforcement agencies. Prior to World War II, reportedly, at least some M97 Riot Guns were converted to trench-gun configuration.

According to Canfield, as of July 1, 1940, there were a total of 21,187 military shotguns in government arsenals, the majority being M97s (Canfield 1997: 75). Other types will be discussed below. As it appeared likely that the United States would enter World War II, in November 1941 a contract was executed for Winchester to produce 1,494 M97 Trench Guns. Springfield Armory also ordered a quantity of spare parts for the M97 from Winchester.

On January 6, 1942, shortly after the Pearl Harbor attack of December 7, 1941, Winchester received a rush order for more M97 and M12 (to be discussed below) Trench Guns. In March 1942, Winchester was given new shotgun contracts calling for the production of both M97 Trench and Riot Guns, as well as longer-barreled training guns. The training guns would generally be used for training aerial gunners to lead targets. Enough M97 Trench and Riot Guns had been produced by March 23, 1943 that contracts were cancelled for further production.

There were some noteworthy differences between the World War II M97 combat shotguns and those from World War I. Among the most notable was that World War II M97s were usually built on takedown models, while World War I examples had been built on solid-frame models. Also noticeable is that the World War II ventilated handguard has four holes instead of the six present on the World War I model, though some guns assembled early in World War II – mostly those from the November 1941 contract – still used the older handguard. Other less obvious differences were also present.

A Marine dog handler on Peleliu, September 23, 1944 reads a message while his Doberman "Devil Dog" waits to his left and his Winchester M12 Trench Gun leans nearby. (NARA)

13

World War II-era M97 and M12 Trench Guns lean against the front of a 1942 Dodge ¾-ton WC51 truck. (Jeff Moeller & Mike Spradlin)

Winchester M12

During World War I, the Ordnance Department had acquired other combat shotguns. After the M97 Trench Gun, probably the most famous US fighting shotgun was Winchester's M12 Trench Gun. Stevens Arms Company had introduced a hammerless slide-action shotgun in 1904, followed by Remington in 1908. To stay competitive, Winchester also needed a hammerless slide-action repeater. Chief Winchester engineer Thomas C. Johnson was given the assignment of developing a hammerless design. It used a tipping bolt that locked into the top of the receiver. Its long receiver housed the bolt throughout the entire operating cycle. This would prove a

The Winchester M12 Trench Gun, which was acquired in small numbers during World War I, and much larger quantities during World War II. (Courtesy of Rock Island Auction Company)

THE M12 EXPOSED

Winchester M12 Trench Gun

1. Bayonet lug
2. Magazine spring
3. Magazine follower
4. Cartridges (up to five) in tubular magazine
5. Action slide
6. Cartridge cut-off
7. Carrier
8. Cross-bolt safety
9. Trigger guard
10. Trigger
11. Carrier spring
12. Buttstock
13. Hammer spring and guide rod
14. Hammer pin
15. Hammer
16. Firing-pin retractor
17. Receiver
18. Breechbolt
19. Firing pin
20. Ejection port
21. Cartridge in chamber
22. Barrel
23. Bead front sight

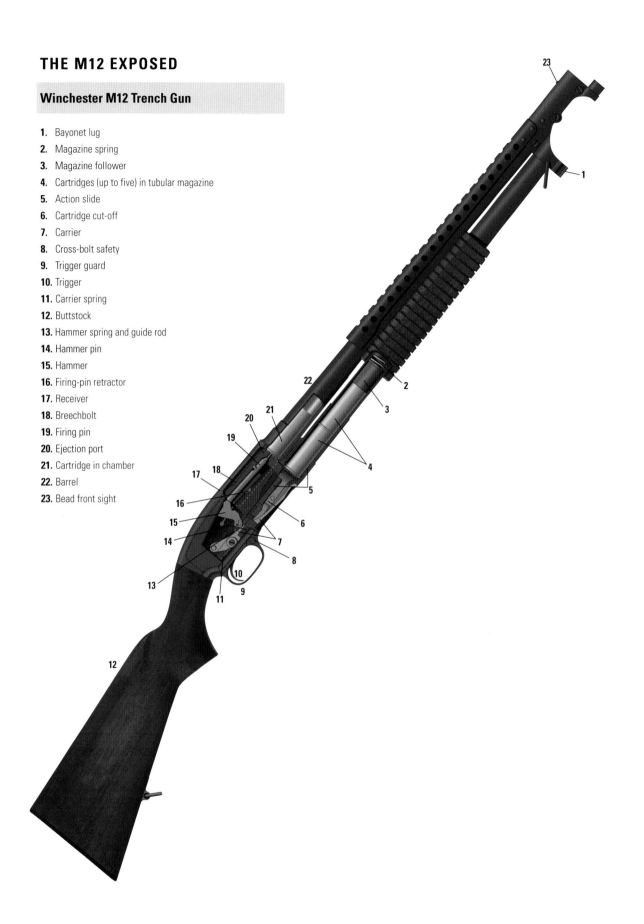

useful feature in military usage as it helped keep debris from entering the action. When introduced in 1912, the M12 was only chambered for the 20-gauge cartridge, but by 1914 it was being offered in 12-gauge. An M12 Riot Gun was introduced in 1918. Magazine capacity was five rounds and like the M97 there was no trigger disconnect, so the M12 could be fired rapidly by just holding back the trigger and operating the forearm.

The US Government also expressed interest in Winchester M12 Riot and Trench Guns for use in World War I. However, Winchester's emphasis on producing the M97 as well as M1917 rifles meant that only a small number of M12s were produced. A few World War I M12 Riot Guns are known, but it seems the M12 Trench Gun was only produced in prototype form. Bruce Canfield reports that Winchester records indicate 600 M12 Riot Guns delivered to the US Government between May 1917 and July 1919 (Canfield 2007: 47).

During World War II, however, the M12 was acquired in substantial numbers. A March 1942 contract with Winchester called for the production of M12 Riot and Trench Guns as well as M97 shotguns. Between April 1, 1942 and March 21, 1944 Winchester delivered 61,014 M12 Trench, Riot, and longer-barreled training guns (Canfield 2007: 90). The largest proportion of these were trench and riot guns. The training guns' barrels were 28–30in long and featured a compensator; they were used for firing at trap or skeet for aerial gunnery training to learn to lead targets. An additional 7,636 M12 shotguns were delivered in 16-gauge (Canfield 1997: 90). Reportedly, many of these were used by defense-plant guards and for other duties within the continental United States. These 16-gauge guns were long-barreled sporting models.

M12 Trench and Riot Guns used the takedown receiver. Barrels were 20in cylinder bore, and on trench models used the same ventilated handguard with four rows of holes as the M97 Trench Gun. The US Marines, especially, liked the M12 and used it in the Pacific, Korea, and Vietnam. The M12 remained a standard US military shotgun through the Vietnam War, though it saw limited use even later. Because the M12 Trench and Riot Guns saw such extensive use, they were frequently arsenal refurbished, which means pristine examples are highly sought by collectors.

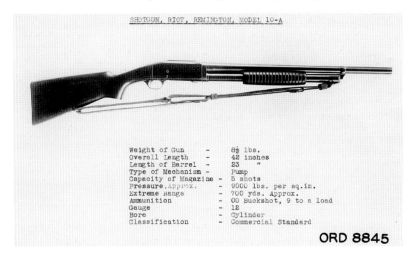

SHOTGUN, RIOT, REMINGTON, MODEL 10-A

Weight of Gun	-	8½ lbs.
Overall Length	-	42 inches
Length of Barrel	-	23 "
Type of Mechanism	-	Pump
Capacity of Magazine	-	5 shots
Pressure, Approx.	-	9000 lbs. per sq.in.
Extreme Range	-	700 yds. Approx.
Ammunition	-	00 Buckshot, 9 to a load
Gauge	-	12
Bore	-	Cylinder
Classification	-	Commercial Standard

ORD 8845

An official Ordnance Department photograph of the Remington M10 Riot Gun, which was acquired in relatively small numbers for service in World War I. (NARA)

Remington M10

To supplement the Winchester Trench and Riot Guns and later to replace them, various other slide-action shotguns were acquired from World War I through the War on Terror. In World War I, to supplement production of the Winchester M97 Trench Gun, Remington was awarded a contract to produce a trench version of its M10 slide-action shotgun. Designed by John Pederson, the M10 was a hammerless design that ejected shells downward from the receiver and had a safety, which could be operated with either hand, at the front of the trigger guard. It had a five-round magazine capacity. (The Winchester M12 owed its tipping bolt-locking system to the M10.) Since Winchester had a patent on the handguard used on its trench guns, Remington developed its own design, consisting of a wooden handguard and separate bayonet adaptor for the M1917 rifle bayonet. One bayonet adaptor designed by Remington would have used the bayonet for the Remington Rolling Block rifle, of which Remington had a substantial supply, but only prototypes were made as the US Government wanted trench guns that used the M1917 bayonet. The M10 Trench Gun also had a longer barrel than the Winchester trench guns, at 23in. However, approximately 1,500 M10 Riot Guns with 20in barrels were delivered to the US Government as well. After World War I, most of the M10 Trench Guns were converted to riot-gun configuration with their barrels shortened to 20in.

The Remington M10 Trench Gun acquired for use during World War I; note the wooden handguard; when using the M1917 bayonet, this allowed the shotgun to be grasped without burning the hand. (NARA)

Remington M31

During World War II the need for shotguns early in the conflict was substantial enough that slide-action shotguns were obtained from other manufacturers besides Winchester. Although the primary military combat shotgun produced by Remington during the war was the M11 semiautomatic, which will be discussed later, just under 9,000 Remington Model 31 (M31) slide-action Riot Guns and training shotguns, were acquired by the US Government during World War II. Though only a few examples saw combat, the M31 was rated as of similar quality to Winchester's M12.

During World War I various experimental shotguns were examined. Shown is a Remington M10 pump-action shotgun with a Russian Mosin-Nagant bayonet adaptor; Remington had produced Mosin-Nagant rifles for Russia prior to the United States' involvement in World War I, and so the company had a stock of Mosin-Nagant bayonets. (NARA)

Stevens M520-30

Far more slide-action fighting shotguns were acquired during World War II from the Savage/Stevens Company. The best-known is the Stevens Model 520-30 (M520-30), dating from 1904 and based on a John

Browning design. A prototype M520 Trench Gun had actually been submitted for consideration during World War I, but the war ended before it was adopted. The original M520 was a hammerless design with a bolt that locked into the top of the receiver. Recoil unlocked the forearm to allow the action to be cycled, or, if the shotgun had not been fired, a slide lock button had to be depressed. The improved M520-30 had a safety located atop the tang of the receiver, allowing it to be easily operated with the thumb of the shooting hand. Production for the M520-30 had actually been discontinued in 1932, but because of slow sales during the Depression quite a few were on hand which were purchased by the US Government in Riot, Trench, and training formats. With a large government order on offer, Stevens began production of the M520-30 again, eventually producing 35,306 military shotguns of all types (Canfield 2007: 94).

During World War II, the Ordnance Department acquired both Stevens M520-30 Riot Guns and Trench Guns. Shown here is an M520-30 Riot Gun. (Courtesy of Rock Island Auction Company)

In addition to M520-30 shotguns, the Ordnance Department also acquired Stevens M620A Riot Guns and Trench Guns. Shown here is an M620A Trench Gun. (Courtesy of Rock Island Auction Company)

Stevens M620A

The Stevens Model 620A (M620A), which had superseded the M520-30, was also purchased for military issue. The M620A used basically the same action as the M520-30, but the receiver had been streamlined to remove the square shape at its rear. Canfield gives a figure of 12,174 M620A Riot, Trench, and training shotguns as being sold to the US Government during World War II (Canfield 2007: 95).

Ithaca M37

Ithaca Arms received a contract for their M37 Riot, Trench, and training guns during 1941 prior to the Pearl Harbor attack. The M37 design was based on the earlier Remington Model 1917 (M17), the patents on which had run out by 1937 when the M37 was introduced. Like the Remington M10 used in World War I, the M37 ejected downward. It was also quite a light shotgun at only 6.3lb in riot-gun format. Although Ithaca delivered 12,433 shotguns of all types to the US Government during the war, only 1,422 were M37 Trench Guns. Many of the other shotguns were obtained early in the war when the US Government was purchasing any shotguns available. The Ordnance Department deemed it more important for Ithaca to produce M1911A1 pistols than trench and riot shotguns, however, so no additional orders were placed. Like the Winchester M97 and M12, the Ithaca M37 did not have a trigger disconnect which would have allowed it to be fired by holding back the trigger and working the action.

While World War II M37 Trench Guns had 20in barrels, most of the M37 Riot Guns delivered to the US Government had 22in barrels. An authentic World War II Ithaca M37 Trench Gun is extremely rare and highly sought after by collectors.

On November 6, 1968 at Dong Tan, Vietnam, MPs load suspected VC onto a truck for transport to the 9th Infantry Division Detainee Collection Point. The shotgun being handed to the MP in the truck appears to be a Stevens M77E. (NARA)

SLIDE-ACTION SHOTGUNS IN KOREA AND VIETNAM

After World War II, many of the shotguns in the military inventory had seen heavy use and were refurbished at various arsenals. Although a variety of shotguns remained in inventory, the three standardized for postwar use were the Winchester M12 Trench Gun, Stevens M520-30 Trench Gun, and Stevens M620A Trench Gun. Nevertheless, during the Korean War M97 Trench Guns also saw service, as did some others.

The jungle fighting in Vietnam created expanded demand for fighting shotguns. In addition to Winchester M97 and M12 Trench Guns and Stevens M520-30 and M620A Trench Guns, which were in armories, a substantial number of additional shotguns were acquired. In November 1962 around 22,000 Ithaca M37 Riot Guns were ordered for the Army of the Republic of Vietnam (ARVN). At least a few of these made it into the hands of US advisors fighting alongside the ARVN. Later, Ithaca M37 Riot Guns and a small number of M37 Trench Guns were also ordered for US troops. The US Navy SEALs were especially fond of the M37. At least some of the SEAL M37s were apparently trench models, as the US Navy had ordered M37 Trench Guns in 1967.

During US Army Ranger training in 1982, a soldier fires an M1200 Trench Gun with folding stock. (NARA)

Stevens M77E

Other slide-action shotguns ordered during the Vietnam War included the Stevens M77E Riot Gun. Between 1963 and 1969 a total of 69,079 M77E Riot Guns were ordered (Canfield 2007: 173). One weakness of the M77E discovered in combat was the somewhat fragile attachment of the stock to the receiver. When the weapon was used in hand-to-hand combat the stock was known to break off.

Winchester M1200

One of the more interesting slide-action combat shotguns used in Vietnam was the Winchester M1200. Introduced in 1964 as a successor to the M12, the M1200 had an aluminum-alloy receiver, which was lighter than the steel receiver of the M12 and which was also more corrosion resistant. Both were appealing features to troops fighting a jungle war. The locking system employed four locking lugs on the bolt, which locked into a steel barrel extension. Another useful feature for a military shotgun was a self-contained trigger group that could be removed as a unit for maintenance. One feature some troops who had used the M12 did not like was the addition of a trigger disconnect on the M1200, which precluded holding the trigger back and pumping for rapid fire.

Some time around 1967–68, Winchester introduced an M1200 Trench Gun in an attempt to gain military orders. Shortly thereafter, Winchester received contracts for M1200 Trench Guns and possibly M1200 Riot Guns. Although the handguard/bayonet mount for the M1200 was similar to that used on the M97 and M12 Trench Guns, there were some differences. For example, the handguard had six rows of holes as on the

The big shotgun in Vietnam: the M79 grenade launcher

The M79 grenade launcher, which saw extremely wide use in Vietnam, is a single-shot break-open design that can fire an array of 40mm grenades. These include buckshot and flechette rounds, which allowed it to be used as a large-bore shotgun. On patrol, an M79 grenadier would often carry a buckshot load in his weapon for use should an enemy patrol be encountered on a trail. Some Special Forces operators used M79s with the barrel and stock cut down and loaded with buckshot as secondary weapons to clear a trail or to help break an ambush.

Two buckshot rounds were available for the M79 – the M576E1 buckshot round and the M576E2 buckshot round. The E1 round contained 20 No 00 buckshot pellets while the E2 round contained 27 pellets. Troops considered the M576E1 round more effective even though it contained fewer buckshot as it used a sabot to keep the pattern tighter, thus putting more hits on target out to 40m (43.7yd). The flechette round available for the M79 contained 45 ten-grain flechettes, but they proved unstable at all but very close ranges and were not normally used.

ABOVE The XM576E1 canister round for the 40mm grenade launcher. It would become standardized as the M576, which fired 20 buckshot pellets. (Jeff Moeller & Mike Spradlin)

World War I trench guns and the unit was parkerized.[3] Probably because the M1917 bayonet was standard for other US military shotguns, the M1200 bayonet lug was also designed for the same bayonet.

Many of the M1200 Trench Guns did not get shipped to Vietnam. Reportedly, some went to National Guard Armories for use during the riots that plagued US cities during the turbulent 1960s. Other M1200 Trench Guns remained in use with US Army units until the 21st century, reportedly being issued in Iraq.

The M870 Mk I was developed late in the Vietnam War for the USMC, though it saw little if any action in that conflict. It was, however, used by the Marines for decades afterward. (Jeff Moeller & Mike Spradlin)

Remington M870

The Remington M870 has been for decades the most popular slide-action combat shotgun with US law-enforcement agencies, as well as foreign government agencies. It has also seen service with US military units. During 1969, a version of the M870 was developed for the USMC to supplement the Corps' aging supply of shotguns. Designated the Model 870 Mk I, this USMC M870 was based on the standard Remington M870 "Wingmaster" with a 21in barrel fitted with a bayonet adaptor for the

3   Parkerizing is a method of protecting a steel surface from corrosion and also increasing wear resistance through applying an electrochemical phosphate conversion coating.

Close-up of the bayonet adaptor on the USMC Remington M870 Mk I. (Jeff Moeller & Mike Spradlin)

M7 bayonet used on the M16 rifle, rifle sights, an extended seven-round magazine tube, and a parkerized finish. In the spring of 1969, Remington was given a contract for 3,230 M870 Mk I shotguns (Canfield 2007: 182). Like the Winchester M1200 Trench Guns, the USMC M870 Mk I shotguns remained in use into the 21st century.

An array of M870 Riot Guns was acquired by the US Navy with 18in and 20in barrels, usually – but not always – parkerized, and typically with extended magazine tubes. The US Air Force (USAF) also used the Remington M870 Riot Gun for base-security units.

SLIDE-ACTION SHOTGUNS AFTER VIETNAM

Mossberg M500 and M590

The Winchester M1200 and Remington M870 slide-action military shotguns remained in US service for decades after the Vietnam War, seeing service during the First Gulf War and Somalia. By the early 1980s, though, slide-action Mossberg shotguns began to enter service. Earliest orders were for the Mossberg M500, which had first been marketed by O. F. Mossberg & Sons in 1961. Employing an alloy receiver, the M500 included other useful features such as a sliding tang safety and twin action bars to help prevent binding during rapid operation of the forearm.

Mossberg developed the M590 primarily for the law-enforcement and military markets. Features included a magazine-tube cap that was easily removable to allow cleaning, or to affix an extension for greater magazine capacity. A M590 Trench Gun was developed as well, with a ventilated handguard and bayonet lug for the M7 bayonet.

In the past, US military shotguns were often adopted quickly due to the exigencies of war. In the case of the Mossberg, however, it had to pass a set of standards (MILSPEC 3443E) developed for slide-action (pump-action) shotguns. These standards included firing 3,000 consecutive rounds with no more than two malfunctions and no parts breaking or becoming unserviceable. Mossberg M500 and M590 shotguns were also subjected to strength tests and operational tests under extreme temperatures, and tested for resistance to corrosives and other chemicals. Original military order Mossbergs had oiled walnut stocks, but after 1986 synthetic stocks became standard.

Mossberg M500 and M590 shotguns of the kind shown here have been in use with the US armed forces for decades. (Martin Floyd)

First orders were for M500 shotguns with 20in barrels and five-round magazines. During 1981, the US Navy acquired 5,085 M500s and the US Coast Guard 800. The next Mossberg contract was in 1984–85 when a combined total of 2,756 M500s were purchased by the US Army and US Navy. In 1987, the USMC ordered 1,331 M590 Trench Guns with extended eight-shot magazines. Subsequent orders for M500 shotguns included those with 14in barrels and folding stocks, which were easier to use for door-breaching and ship-boarding operations. All Mossberg military-contract shotguns incorporated sling-swivels.

Mossberg M500 and M590 shotguns saw service in Operation *Desert Storm* and continued use in Afghanistan and Iraq. Some of the shotguns used for door breaching have been fitted with pistol-grip stocks to allow their use in tight spaces and also to allow them to be carried more readily as an adjunct to an M4 carbine.

Members of the USMC undergoing breaching training with the Mossberg M590 shotgun. (USMC)

SELF-LOADING SHOTGUNS

As early as World War I, the US Government also acquired some semiautomatic shotguns for military use. In fact, even before World War I, some Remington semiautomatic shotguns had been used in the Philippines and had performed well. Although semiautomatic designs are more sensitive to the cartridge being used, which can affect reliability, they offer some advantages; the most obvious is that the operator does not have to move his support arm to chamber a round. Each round is chambered automatically. This allows the semiautomatic combat shotgun to be fired more effectively in confined space or when prone. Also, should one of his arms be injured, the operator can continue to fight more effectively.

The US Ordnance Department experimented with semiautomatic designs as early as World War I. Shown is a Browning Automatic with full-length wooden handguard and an offset bayonet mount. (NARA)

Remington M11

During World War I, at least a few Remington M11 recoil-operated semiautomatics were purchased, including some riot guns. Most seem to have been used for guarding prisoners in the United States, or possibly for aerial-gunnery practice. Designed by John Browning, the Remington Autoloading Shotgun, designated the M11 after 1911, was virtually identical to the Browning shotgun marketed by Fabrique Nationale (FN). With a 20in barrel and four-round magazine, the Remington riot version was marketed prior to World War I.

During World War I, Remington worked on developing a "trench" version of the M11. However, since the M11 used a recoiling barrel, developing a method for mounting a bayonet offered a problem, as punching forward with a bayonet and striking a target would likely cause the barrel to move backward, unlocking and ejecting the shell in the chamber – or, even worse, partially ejecting the shell, causing a jam. To solve this problem, Remington developed a jacket that was fitted around the barrel and mounted the bayonet. A wooden handguard was also developed to fit over the jacket and prevent the hand from being burned when employing the bayonet after the shotgun had been fired. The "Remington Automatic Trench Gun" was ready by the fall of 1918, but by that time the war was nearly over, and it never went into production.

A Remington "Sportsman" version of the M11 in riot-gun configuration purchased by the US Government during World War II. (Author)

The Remington M11 was purchased in substantial numbers for World War II, with just over 60,000 riot and training versions being delivered.

There were actually two riot versions of this model delivered – the M11 and the "Sportsman," an M11 with only a two-round magazine and a slightly different forearm. The standard M11 Riot Gun had a four-round magazine capacity. Most or all of the training versions went to the US Navy and were mounted in naval gun mounts to train troops in aerial gunnery. Some of the training M11 and "Sportsman" shotguns had Cutts Compensators mounted.[4]

Savage M720

One other semiautomatic riot model was adopted in World War II – the Savage M720, which is very similar in appearance and function to the Remington M11. As with the M11 and "Sportsman," the M720 Riot Gun had a 20in barrel and, like the M11, a four-round magazine capacity. According to Canfield, a total of 14,527 M720 Riot Guns and training guns were delivered during 1943 and 1944 (Canfield 2007: 95).

Prototypes: the Atchisson and the SOW

During the Korean and Vietnam Wars, the United States still relied on slide-action shotguns; however, during the Vietnam War interest in an auto-loading shotgun with a large magazine capacity inspired experimentation with different designs. One interesting design was the Atchisson full-automatic 12-gauge shotgun, which was fed from a 20-round drum magazine. Designed to have dimensions and appearance similar to the M16 rifle, and using a straight-blowback action, the Atchisson was available in prototype form in 1972. To save development costs, some parts from other weapons were used – the M1918 Browning Automatic Rifle's trigger assembly, for example. It proved surprisingly controllable in full-automatic fire. However, the Atchisson never went into production.

Another design that generated some interest during the Vietnam era was the "US Naval Special Operations Weapon" (SOW). Developed beginning in 1970 at the Naval Surface Warfare Center at Dahlgren, Virginia, the SOW was a select-fire 12-gauge shotgun that could fire from either a 20-round double-column magazine or a belt. To enable better control on full-automatic fire, the SOW was equipped with a forward pistol grip on the left side and a collapsible stock. Once again, the SOW did not really progress past the prototype stage.

Remington M7188

The one full-automatic shotgun that actually made it into combat was the Remington M7188. Remington engineers evaluated feedback from troops fighting in Vietnam and began work on a semiautomatic shotgun tailored to the combat environment in Vietnam. Based on studies of the British and Commonwealth counterinsurgency campaign in Malaya, it was determined that delivery of the maximum number of rounds on a target per contact could best be accomplished with a full-automatic shotgun.

4   The Cutts Compensator is a device that lessens muzzle climb.

A member of the 24th Marine Expeditionary Unit fires the M1014 semiautomatic shotgun. (USMC)

Remington began work on the full-automatic M7188 based on the Remington M1100 (Swearengen 1978: 328). A semiautomatic version, the M7180, was also developed.

As development of the M7188 progressed, Remington developed a handguard and bayonet adaptor that would take the M7 bayonet. By 1966, Remington had prototype versions available that had 20in barrels, rifle sights, sandblasted phosphate finish, extended magazines holding six or seven rounds, and sling-swivels. Prototypes in semiautomatic were the same except they did not have select-fire capability. The M7188 Mk I version as prepared for military sales had a 20in barrel with an extended magazine tube to take seven rounds, Remington-designed ventilated handguard and bayonet adaptor for the M7 bayonet, rifle sights, sling-swivels, and parkerized finish on external parts. Variations included the Mk II, which had a standard shotgun bead instead of rifle sights; the Mk III, which did not have the ventilated handguard or bayonet adaptor but did have rifle sights; and the Mk IV, which was like the Mk III but with a shotgun bead sight. Other versions such as the Mk V and Mk VI did not have the extended magazine tube.

Both the M7180 Mk I and the M7188 Mk I were tested extensively by the USMC, but the Corps chose the Remington M870 Mk I slide-action instead. A small number of M7188 shotguns – reportedly six, but some sources state more than a dozen – did see combat in Vietnam with the US Navy SEALs, but were found very hard to control on full-automatic fire and had too small a magazine capacity (Swearengen 1978: 337). The M7188 also proved highly sensitive to dirt or debris in the action, which could cause malfunctions.

Benelli M1014

It was as a result of the Joint Service Combat Shotgun project, however, that the United States got its first widely issued semiautomatic combat shotgun. On May 4, 1998 the US Army Armaments Research Development and Engineering Center at Picatinny Arsenal, New Jersey, issued the following official requirements for a semiautomatic "Joint Service Combat Shotgun":

A member of the US Army firing an M4 carbine with the M26 MASS mounted. (US Army)

- Capable of semiautomatic operation.
- Capable of firing standard DoD 2.75-inch, 12-gauge No 00 buckshot, and other shot shells and slug ammunition.
- Have a maximum effective range of at least 40 meters [43.7yd] with the DoD standard 2.75-inch No 00 buckshot ammunition, and 100–125 meters [109.4–136.7yd] with slug ammunition.
- Have a length up to 41.75 inches and be capable of reconfiguration to 36 inches or less.
- Weigh no more than 8.5 pounds (six pounds desired) unloaded.
- Be equipped with Low Light Level iron sights and a standard U.S. Military accessory mounting rail integral to the upper receiver, to permit use of other sight enhancement devices. (Quoted in Olive Drab n.d.)

Various firms submitted designs for testing, with the Benelli M4 model the winner of the trials. In February 1999, Heckler & Koch, USA, at that time the US distributor for Benelli, received a contract for the M4, which was initially designated the XM1014 Joint Service Combat Shotgun.

As adopted, the XM1014 was a gas-operated, semiautomatic 12-gauge with an 18.5in barrel and a conventional magazine tube holding six

The USAF M6 Aircrew Survival Weapon

The M6 Aircrew Survival Weapon was never really intended for use as a combat weapon. Instead, aircrew were normally armed with .38 Special revolvers for that mission. The M6 was intended primarily to take small game if the airmen had to bail out over wilderness terrain.

A combination gun with a .22 Hornet barrel on top and a .410 shotgun barrel below, the M6 was produced by Ithaca Gun Company for the USAF. (Developed in the late 1920s at Springfield Armory and produced by Winchester in 1930, the .22 Hornet was the first small-bore high-velocity cartridge marketed in the United States: it is especially suited to killing small game as it reaches over 2,600ft/sec and offers a very flat trajectory.) The M6 had 14in barrels and could fold in half for storage. A firing-pin selector allowed the user to choose whether to fire the rifle or shotgun barrel. The stock was designed so that nine rounds of .22 Hornet ammunition and four rounds of .410 shot shells could be stored in a compartment. Since Cold War-era US bomber crews often operated over Arctic areas, the M6 had a squeeze bar trigger system which could be readily operated when wearing heavy mittens.

Downed airmen were trained to avoid contact with the enemy if behind the lines, so either the revolver or the M6 would only have been used in extreme circumstances, but the .22 Hornet round was entirely capable of killing an enemy, and at close range a .410 shotgun blast would do a lot of damage as well.

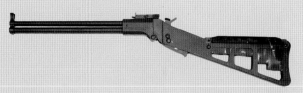

ABOVE The M6 Aircrew Survival Weapon, which combined a .22 Hornet rifle barrel with a .410 shotgun barrel, was intended primarily to take small game, but it could be used against an enemy if necessary. (NARA)

ABOVE The M6 Aircrew Survival Weapon is shown here folded for compact storage. (NARA)

rounds. The shotgun's design and its easily operated cocking handle allowed the action to be cycled manually when "less-lethal" anti-riot rounds,[5] which would not cycle the semiautomatic action, were used. The XM1014 was also designed for extreme reliability with various redundant features such as dual gas ports, pistons, and cylinders. It could also be disassembled for maintenance with no tools. An adjustable "Ghost Ring" (large fast-acquisition aperture) and front post offer good sighting capability, and there is a Picatinny rail for mounting optical sights. Many collapsible stocks for shotguns are uncomfortable when firing because of the shotgun's recoil, but the XM1014 featured a very useful stock that incorporated a pistol grip, a cheek piece, and a thick recoil pad. The adjustable stock allowed the XM1014 to be used at close quarters and also to be fitted to a soldier or Marine wearing body armor.

Once adopted, the shotgun was designated the M1014. The first contract for the M1014 was awarded in 1999 for the USMC, which ordered 3,977 (Canfield 2007: 206). Although the author has seen references to a total of 20,000 M1014 shotguns being ordered for all branches of the US armed forces (but primarily the USMC), he has not been able to confirm that number. As the first user, the USMC was given supervision of the further development of the M1014 for all services.

5   "Less-lethal" is the term used for munitions not intended to kill, for use in riot situations. Though not intended to kill, less-lethal munitions can kill if the rioter is struck in certain vulnerable areas, has respiratory issues that can be affected by gas, etc.

M26 MASS

Although the M1014 is the most recent stand-alone shotgun adopted by the US armed forces, the M26 Modular Accessory Shotgun System (MASS), which is designed to attach to an M4 or M16 much as does an M203 grenade launcher, offers the option of retaining the carbine or rifle but also having a shotgun for close-quarters combat, less-lethal projectiles, or breaching without having to carry a second weapon.

Requirements for the XM26 MASS were first issued in 1997. The M26 MASS was developed by C-MORE Systems of Manassas, Virginia, and tested by the US Army Armaments Research Development and Engineering Center at Picatinny Arsenal, New Jersey. In 2008, the US Army announced that it would acquire 35,000 of the systems. Units began entering service in 2010 with the XVIII Airborne Corps. The M26 MASS employs a straight-pull bolt action and takes three- or five-round detachable box magazines. The unit may be detached from the carbine or rifle and with a stock added can function as a stand-alone shotgun as well.

With Mossberg slide-actions, Benelli M1014 semiautomatics, and M26 MASS units in their armories, US military units have a versatile array of shotguns to perform their missions. More than a century after US troops acquired slide-action M97s to fight Moro terrorists, the United States continues to find the shotgun a valuable weapon against 21st-century terrorists. Development of the fighting shotgun for the US armed forces will continue as new missions arise.

USE
"A frightful weapon to face"

THE INDIAN WARS TO THE PUNITIVE EXPEDITION

Although the shotgun has been used as a combat weapon in the United States since the establishment of the colonies, for the purpose of this book the emphasis will be on those shotguns specifically purchased for military use. One of the more interesting early US military shotguns was used along with the M1873 Trapdoor Springfield. Designated the Springfield Model 1881 (M1881), a 20-gauge shotgun based on the M1873 was issued for use by troops to forage for small game. Nevertheless, it could be used for close-range combat: it may well have been so used during the Indian Wars. Reportedly, US Army units in Alaska continued to use the M1881 to take game until 1906, years after the M1873 rifle had been supplanted by the M1892 Krag and then the M1903 Springfield.

Other shotguns, including the Spencer Repeating Shotgun and Winchester M93 shotgun, were purchased in small numbers for guarding prisoners or for testing. It was the introduction of the M97, combined with the counterinsurgency campaign in the Philippines, which helped the shotgun prove itself as an infantry weapon. The difficulty in stopping fanatical *Juramentados* with the anemic Colt .38 revolvers in use by US troops was a major impetus in the design and adoption of the .45-caliber Colt M1911 pistol. Even the M1892 Krag rifle was not a sure stopper of a *Juramentado* attack. As a result, the US Army purchased hundreds of Winchester M97s for use in the Philippines. Not all started their existence as riot guns: reportedly many were longer-barreled shotguns shortened to 20in barrels. The guns were 12-gauge, cylinder-bore weapons.

There are numerous reports of the effectiveness of the M97 in the Philippines. James Arnold gives a good description of the stopping effect of the M97. In July 1909, US troops tracked down the Moro pirate Jikiri and cornered him on the tiny island of Patian. Jikiri had successfully

attacked ships of the pearling fleet and had boasted that he would run *Juramentado* in the streets of Jolo on the island of Sulu. (The Bates Treaty of 1899 had acknowledged American control of Sulu. The inability to defend Jolo would have severely undermined American authority.) Jikiri's exploits made him a figure around whom Moros could rally, and killing or capturing him was a high priority. Jikiri and a small band of followers took refuge in a cave:

The M1881 Springfield "Forager" shotgun in 20-gauge was designed to allow troops to hunt for game but could be used for combat if necessary. (Martin Floyd)

> … The Americans methodically surrounded the crater, brought up heavy weapons, and bombarded the cave over the course of three days. After a pair of Navy Colt automatics blasted the cave opening at point blank range, the besiegers concluded that nothing inside could remain alive. On the morning of July 4, a mixed force of U.S. Cavalry troopers and Navy sailors cautiously advanced toward the mouth of the cave. Suddenly, seven kris-wielding[6] warriors emerged, led by Jikiri himself. The surprised Americans delivered an ineffective fire. Jikiri advanced through the fire, grabbed Lieutenant Arthur Wilson by the hair, and was about to decapitate him when Lieutenant Joe Baer rushed up, jammed his 12-gauge Winchester pump shotgun against Jikiri's head and blew off the top of his skull.
>
> An eye-gouging, kris- and bayonet stabbing melee ensued during which Baer killed three more Moros with his sawed off shotgun while a sailor skewered a fourth with his bayonet. The cavalry troopers shot down the remaining two Moros. The melee had lasted some ten seconds. When it was over, Jikiri and his outlaws were dead alongside three slain Americans. Nineteen Americans were wounded during Jikiri's last stand. So died the last of the Sulu Sea buccaneers. (Arnold 2011: 186–87)

The speed with which Baer managed to kill four Moros offers a good testament to how fast the slide action of the M97 could be operated by holding the trigger back and working the action. Arnold also mentions the precautions taken at remote camps located in the middle of Moro territory, camps that often contained the wives and children of American officers: "To help defend remote camps, Bliss ordered that each regular company have at least four repeating shotguns. Bliss explained that soldiers had found them invaluable in high grass and underbrush because 'they stop men in their tracks.' But neither exceptional vigilance, extensive fortifications, nor weaponry stopped all Moro infiltration" (Arnold 2011: 201).

6   A *kris* is a dagger with an asymmetrical, wavy blade.

The US-led Philippine Constabulary was also armed with shotguns, not because of the shotgun's effectiveness but because of distrust among elements of the US hierarchy of the Moro members of the Constabulary and the reluctance to arm them with rifles. Most "Constabulary Shotguns" were single-shot Remington 12-gauges, most likely the M93 model, though it was not stated in government orders. Between June 1900 and April 1902, orders were placed for 5,450 of the Remington shotguns with 28in barrels. Though members of the Constabulary were armed with only single-shot shotguns, they were also armed with a version of the M1878 Colt .45 double-action revolver.

In his history of the Philippine Constabulary, Vic Hurley offers an example of one of the Constabulary shotguns in use. On February 24, 1902, Inspector Henry Knauber of the Philippine Constabulary was riding with two enlisted men in Cavite Province when they were ambushed by insurgents:

Knauber is thinking, possibly, that the place is admirably suited for an ambush. He rides cautiously, his outmoded Remington shotgun at the alert ...

... The whine of a Mauser bullet salutes them at a bend of the trail. Smoke drifts across the tasseled top *cogon* [grass] as the shotgun in Knauber's hands blasts at a whirling shadow that rises from the grass. A wild shriek, blood-curdling and shrill, sounds in the depths of the grass as eight insurgent soldiers of the disorganized Filipino army rush the Constabulary detail ...

... The three Constabulary soldiers rise to meet the rush of eight bolomen who are commanded by one "Captain" Julian Ramos. There is a blur of sound and movement as men face the greatest adventure of all.

Teeth and shotgun butt and bolo edge and bare hands come into play that day, and when fifteen frenzied minutes have passed the jungle becomes silent again but for the clatter of the indignant monkeys and the protests of the noisy parrots. (Hurley 2011: 31–33)

There seems to have been an attempt to arm at least some members of the Philippine Constabulary with M97 shotguns. According to Hurley, "Orders were hastily placed in America for 1,000 Winchester shotguns and a suitable quantity of brass shells. Also ordered were 5,000 Colt revolvers, caliber .45. (This to satisfy the Army, who at the time was using .38-caliber revolvers.)" (Hurley 2011: 65). However, as it transpired, Winchester did not have enough repeating shotguns on hand to fill the order, so the

Technical manual specifications on the M19 US shotgun shell. (Author's collection)

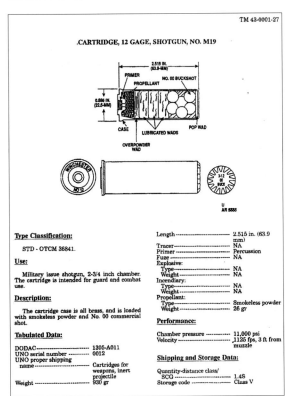

TM 43-0001-27

.CARTRIDGE, 12 GAGE, SHOTGUN, NO. M19

Type Classification:

STD - OTCM 36841.

Use:

Military issue shotgun, 2-3/4 inch chamber. The cartridge is intended for guard and combat use.

Description:

The cartridge case is all brass, and is loaded with smokeless powder and No. 00 commercial shot.

Tabulated Data:

DODAC 1305-A011
UNO serial number 0012
UNO proper shipping
name .... Cartridges for weapons, inert projectile
Weight .... 930 gr

Length .... 2.515 in. (63.9 mm)
Tracer .... NA
Primer .... Percussion
Fuze .... NA
Explosive:
Type .... NA
Weight .... NA
Incendiary:
Type .... NA
Weight .... NA
Propellant:
Type .... Smokeless powder
Weight .... 26 gr

Performance:

Chamber pressure .... 11,000 psi
Velocity .... 1125 fps, 3 ft from muzzle

Shipping and Storage Data:

Quantity-distance class/
SCG 1.4S
Storage code .... Class V

Military shotgun loads: the Philippine Insurrection to World War II

During the Philippine Insurrection and much of World War I, commercial 00 buckshot loads in paper cases, 25 to the box, were purchased for issuance with riot and trench shotguns. Late in World War I, in an attempt to address the problems with paper shells, brass 00 buckshot rounds were obtained from Winchester and Remington. It is likely that Winchester shells had what is sometimes called the "sawtooth" crimp because of the "teeth" that were bent over the retaining cardboard disc. On this disc was printed "3½" to designate the drams of powder (or with smokeless powder the dram equivalent) and "00 Buck" to designate the projectiles.

Between World War I and World War II, there were enough shotgun shells still in government stores that no orders were placed until the 1930s when some brass 00 buckshot cartridges were ordered from Winchester (boxes may have been marked Western Cartridge Company, which had acquired Winchester in 1931). In 1940, new contracts for paper-cased buckshot loads were granted. After 1942, contracts called for case heads of plated steel and paper cases that were waterproofed. Primarily for use in shotguns issued for guard duty, which would be constantly loaded and unloaded, some contracts were also granted for all brass shells.

As in World War I, however, problems arose with the paper-cased shells, especially in the Pacific. As a result, late in 1943, the Ordnance Department gave contracts to Remington and Winchester for all-brass 00 buckshot loads. Millions of rounds of brass shotgun shells were delivered in 1944. Early in 1945, the Ordnance Department designated the brass buckshot loads for overseas use only, while paper cartridges would continue to be used for guard

duty in the United States. On March 29, 1945 the all-brass 00 buckshot shell was approved as standard for US military usage and designated "Shell, Shotgun, All Brass, 12-Gauge, No. 00 Buck, M19."

After adoption of the M19 round, large orders were placed with Remington Arms Company, the ammunition to be packed in ten-round cartons. A dozen ten-round cartons were packed in green sealed metal M10 cans, with two of the cans packed into an M12 wooden crate for overseas shipment.

ABOVE Two of the brass shotgun shells of the type acquired during World War I and World War II. The one at left has the sawtooth crimp, which may indicate it was produced at the end of World War I or just after. (Author)

ABOVE Various boxes of World War II-era paper buckshot cartridges acquired for US military use. (Jeff Moeller & Mike Spradlin)

LEFT World War II M19 brass cartridges like these were primarily acquired for the USMC in the Pacific after paper shells were found to be unreliable in the damp jungle fighting: the same problem that had arisen with paper shells in World War I. (Author)

Constabulary did not receive the very effective M97. Hurley discusses the armament of the Constabulary by 1904: "The ordnance records show on hand 7,370 Springfield rifles, single-shot; 2,251 Remington rifles, also single-shot; 4,072 shotguns, mostly single-shot, but included were a few repeating pump guns; 5,129 Colt .45-caliber revolvers, double-action; 2,094 Colt .45-caliber revolvers, single-action; and 600 Colt .41-caliber revolvers" (Hurley 2011: 166–67).

Note that by 1904, the Constabulary had received rifles, but these were M1892 Krags, which were being superseded by the M1903 Springfield. Hurley points out that among US regular troops the shotgun continued to be one of the most effective weapons against the Moros:

On October 17, 1911, one Moro, armed with a *barong*[7] and spear, ran the gauntlet of sentries of the 2nd Cavalry, stationed at Lake Seit. As the

7   A *barong* is an edged weapon with a leaf-shaped, single-edged blade.

mad Mohammedan hurtled down the company street, the target of fire from all directions, his eyes were fixed on Sergeant Oswald Homilius as the first object of attack. The Sergeant went down, pierced through with the spear. Riddled then with bullets, the Moro turned methodically to the nearest American soldiers. Racing into point-blank fire, he cut down four American troopers with his *barong* before Lieutenant Coppock was able to deliver the full charge of a shotgun at close range. (Hurley 2011: 315)

At least some M97s accompanied US troops on the Punitive Expedition into Mexico in 1916. These were most likely from the same acquisition as those that went to the Philippines. General John Pershing who led this expedition had seen the devastating effect of the shotgun during his service in the Philippines, and, according to Thomas Swearengen, Pershing equipped some of his cavalrymen with M97 Riot Guns. Reportedly, they proved very effective, to the extent that some cavalrymen preferred them to their rifles (Swearengen 1978: 9).

WORLD WAR I

Pershing, who commanded the American Expeditionary Forces (AEF) during World War I, continued his advocacy of the combat shotgun in France. According to Swearengen:

> When the United States entered World War I in 1917, General John J. Pershing was given command of the American Expeditionary Forces. Among his early acts was a request for shotguns with which to arm his troops. His instincts told him that it would be ideal for trench raids, patrolling, guarding prisoners, and fending off enemy attacks, as well as for making assaults on enemy trenches and machine gun nests. His insight into the adaptability of shotguns for trench warfare proved to be quite accurate. (Swearengen 1978: 9)

To be more suitable for trench fighting, it was determined that the shotgun needed the capability of mounting a bayonet. As a result, Winchester and Springfield Armory worked together to develop a combination handguard/bayonet adaptor for the M97 Riot Gun. This device was designated the "Type W." The M97 Trench Gun proved very popular among US troops, who appreciated its effectiveness at close quarters.

The Germans, however, were horrified at facing the trench shotgun. On September 19, 1918 the Swiss Government presented Robert Lansing, the US Secretary of State, with a cablegram containing the following diplomatic protest by the German Government:

> The German Government protests against the use of shotguns by the American Army and calls attention to the fact that according to the law of war (*Kriegsrecht*) every [US] prisoner [of war] found to have in his possession such guns or ammunition belonging thereto forfeits his life. This protest is based upon article 23(e) of the Hague convention

[sic] respecting the laws and customs of war on land. Reply by cable is required before October 1, 1918. (Quoted in Parks 1997: 19)

This protest was based at least in part on the capture of two American soldiers – one on July 21 and the other on September 11 – who were armed with M97 Trench Guns loaded with No 00 buckshot. After receiving the protest, the Judge Advocate General of the Army, Brigadier General Samuel T. Ansell, responded on September 26:

US troops at Issoudon, France, train with the M97 Trench Gun during June 1918. (NARA)

Article 23(e) simply calls for comparison between the injury or suffering caused and the necessities of warfare. It is legitimate to kill the enemy and as many of them, and as quickly, as possible ... It is to be condemned only when it wounds, or does not kill immediately, in such a way as to produce suffering that has no reasonable relation to the killing or placing the man out of action for an effective period. The shotgun, although an ancient weapon, finds its class or analogy, as to purpose and effect, in many modern weapons. The dispersion of the shotgun [pellets] ... is adapted to the necessary purpose of putting out of action more than one of the charging enemy with each shot of the gun; and in this respect it is exactly analogous to shrapnel shell discharging a multitude of small [fragments] or a machine gun discharging a spray of ... bullets. The diameter of the bullet is scarcely greater than that of a rifle or machine gun. The weight of it is very much less. And, in both size and weight, it is less than the ... [fragments] of a shrapnel shell ... Obviously a pellet the size of a .32-caliber bullet, weighing only enough to be effective at short ranges, does not exceed the limit necessary for putting a man immediately *hors de combat*.

   The only instances even where a shotgun projectile causes more injury to any one enemy soldier than would a hit by a rifle bullet are instances where the enemy soldier has approached so close to the shooter that he is struck by more than one of the nine ... [No 00 buckshot projectiles] contained in the cartridge. This, like the effect of the dispersing of ... [fragments] from a shrapnel shell, is permissible either in behalf of greater effectiveness or as an unavoidable incident of the use of small scattering projectiles for the necessary purpose of increasing [the] likelihood of killing a number of enemies. (Quoted in Parks 1997: 18)

A World War I-era Winchester M97 Trench Gun. (Courtesy of Rock Island Auction Service)

After receiving Brigadier General Ansell's memorandum, Secretary of State Lansing provided the following reply to the Government of Germany:

> [The] ... provision of the Hague convention, cited in the protest, does not ... forbid the use of this ... weapon ... [I]n view of the history of the shotgun as a weapon of warfare, and in view of the well-known effects of its present use, and in the light of a comparison of it with other weapons approved in warfare, the shotgun ... cannot be the subject of legitimate or reasonable protest. (Quoted in Parks 1997: 20)

American shooters writing to American firearms publications had their own scathing commentary on the German complaints. For example, a July 27, 1918 commentary in *Arms and the Man* magazine leaves no doubt that Americans found German claims of brutality disingenuous at best:

> The Hun with his spiked "morning-star" bludgeon, his convulsion-producing poison gases, his death traps which he leaves in abandoned trenches, his epidemic breeding disease germs, and his torpedoes which make no distinction between ship of battle and ship of mercy, has suddenly discovered that the most barbarous weapon of all the ages is being used against him.
>
> According to dispatches from The Hague, the German newspapers are considerably upset over stories received through Switzerland that a large number of American troops have been supplied with sawed-off shotguns for close fighting. The *Cologne Gazette*, in commenting upon the report denounces "America's barbarism" and assumes that "tommy-hawks and scalping knives will soon make their appearance on the American front." The newspaper warns German troops that the Americans are not "honorable warriors." The *Weser Zeitung* says that the barbarous shotguns have been served out not because they are likely to be effective but because the ill-trained Americans cannot use rifles and are badly supplied with machine guns.

Close-up of the bayonet mount for the Winchester M97 Trench Gun. (Author)

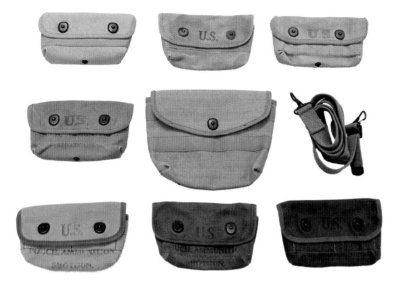

An array of shotgun pouches for US shotgun ammunition. The larger pouch in the center was carried over the shoulder using the strap next to it and was used in World War I. Usually designated the M1918 pouch, it held 32 rounds. Other pouches are belt pouches and include at top left the M1921 pouch, which held 12 rounds. The two other pouches at top and the two to the left of the M1918 are examples of the M1938 pouch widely used during World War II and Korea. The two at bottom right are later versions of the M1938 pouch. (Jeff Moeller & Mike Spradlin)

It is gratifying to learn that the German newspaper man, ostensibly at least, regards the use of the shotgun with horror. It is to be hoped that the German people and the German soldiers will regard these utterances as being sincere and that they will have firmly fixed in their minds the truth which is that the sawed-off shotgun will be a frightful weapon to face […]

If given a choice, the average American soldier would prefer to fight with the weapon for which he has a natural aptitude – the rifle. Yet if he can kill more Germans with the sawed-off shotgun and its exterminating load of buckshot, such talk as that in the *Cologne Gazette* will not deter him. The American soldier has been brought face to face with an unpleasant task, yet one which must be done once and for all. Therefore the United States soldier may confidently be expected to follow the advice of the old gray French Field Marshal – *"Kill Germans."*

In the meantime, the comity of nations which has been bludgeoned by the spiked "morning star," strangled by poison vapors, and racked by the torpedoes which have sunk hospital ships, will undoubtedly survive the spectacle of the highly efficient, Hun-exterminating sawed-off military shotgun. (Anon 1918a: 348)

In October 1918, another reader wrote to the same magazine:

It is distinctly to the credit of the United States Government that Germany's representations seeking to eliminate the use of the military shotgun and her threats of reprisals have been met by a prompt and complete refusal to accede to the Hun's demand.

Secretary Lansing's reply to the German's note will leave no opportunity for even the oblique methods employed by Teutonic reasoning to misunderstand or to remain longer in ignorance of the fact that America will abandon no justifiable implement of war in the work of conquering the Hun.

Remington M10 Trench Guns were also acquired for use during World War I. (Jeff Moeller & Mike Spradlin)

Germany is also rapidly learning that American manhood, plus American marksmanship, plus American weapons, is a combination which spells for the Kaiser's armies complete defeat. Her efforts to take refuge behind the provisions of the Hague convention, which she has so brutally and consistently violated, is one of the strongest bits of evidence that the reports of allied successes from the Western Front are not unfounded propaganda, and that the tactics which are now being employed can be counted upon to ultimately bring the Hun to his knees.

There is a grain of humor in the fact that Germany's protest against the use of the military shotgun should be based upon that Hague provision which especially forbids any belligerent "to employ arms, projections or materials calculated to cause unnecessary suffering." There is little likelihood of suffering on the part of any of the Kaiser's baby-killers after he has stopped a charge from one of the trench shotguns. The chief suffering occasioned by the new American weapon would seem to be mental anguish on the part of the German military leaders, who know with what wholesome fear the German regards the sawed-off scattergun. As for the soldier himself, the shotgun puts him as far beyond all suffering as would his own poison vapors, his liquid fire, the death traps which he leaves in abandoned dugouts, and any one of the other score of last-ditch methods which he is employing to the limit in his extremity in a vain hope that they will react upon the morale of the Allies. (Anon 1918c: 48)

Although General Pershing is generally credited with providing the impetus for adoption of the shotgun for use by the AEF, the Trapshooting Editor of *Baseball* magazine had also written letters to the War Department touting the value of the shotgun for trench combat. In the July 1918 issue, Samuel Wesley Long rather jingoistically describes the new trench shotgun:

The new trench gun is, elementally speaking, a comparatively short automatic shotgun of the "pump" variety capable of sending fifty-four gleaming little globes of 00 buckshot, each about the size of a .32 caliber bullet, all over the anatomy of as many of the Kaiser's six sons as could be crowded into an area measuring nine feet horizontally and about three feet vertically.

Attached to the single barreled shotgun is a bayonet. Also the bayonet is long enough to penetrate beautifully, smoothly and delightfully even a Teutonic waistline, especially as waistlines made in Germany measure these days. The bayonet takes the new shotgun out of the sporting arms class; in fact the shotgun is not manufactured for sporting purposes, but is a trench gun, designed and made solely for the American Army abroad.

Whether the suggestion to adopt the shotgun in warfare came from General Pershing or BASEBALL MAGAZINE is of minor importance; the thing of moment is the fact that a new method of stopping the Huns has been developed. However, BASEBALL MAGAZINE takes a measure of pride in the realization that the campaign which it has conducted to gain recognition for the "scatter gun" has not been without results. (Long 1918: 307)

A close-up view of the Remington M10 Trench Gun's bayonet mount and wooden handguard. (Jeff Moeller & Mike Spradlin)

Anthony Saunders offers his views on the shotgun's use in the trenches. He does not seem to grasp, however, that Americans have a long tradition of using the shotgun as a close-combat weapon and would have felt quite comfortable using it in the trenches:

Some British raiders might have armed themselves with sawn-off shotguns. Clearly, each gun would have been bespoke, the modifications being carried out at Royal Engineer workshop facilities or possibly ordnance repair workshops and such a weapon would have been used by the officer who owned it. Major Stephen Midgley of the Australian 5th Light Horse certainly used a double-barrelled shotgun at Gallipoli until told to stop. The British and Australian use of shotguns was unsanctioned and it is unlikely that higher command was aware of their use. While it is true that the US military used shotguns to some extent on the Western Front, there is little to suggest they were employed specifically on trench raids in 1917 or 1918. Nevertheless, the German troops feared these "trench guns". The American weapon was not a locally modified civilian gun but a weapon specifically adapted by Winchester for trench warfare, with a pump action and a bayonet attachment. It had a shorter barrel than a civilian shotgun and a six-round magazine. The cartridges contained 7–9 pellets of hardened 00-gauge shot, devastating at short range. (Saunders 2012: 125)

Although Saunders states that the shotgun was not used "specifically" in trench raids, tradition has it that Americans used it very effectively in raiding trenches and even more so in repelling German raiders. In regards to his point about the European armies not using the shotgun, Paul Jenkins speculates that one reason for the lack of effective military shotguns from Europe was that European shotguns of the time were designed for lighter loads than the American shotguns, which were often used to hunt big game using buckshot (Jenkins 1935: 15).

Bo Barbour offers one example of a US sergeant using his trench gun to good effect during World War I: "On 27 September 1918, Sergeant Fred

Lloyd, using a Model 97, advanced alone into a German-held village and began methodically clearing the village, rapidly pumping and firing the shotgun as he moved. He finally collapsed with exhaustion after flushing and routing thirty German soldiers" (Barbour 2003). Another soldier who used his shotgun to such good effect that he won a Congressional Medal of Honor was Sergeant Lloyd M. Seibert of Company F, 364th Infantry, 91st Division. On September 26, 1918, near Epinonville, France, as stated in his medal citation:

> Suffering from illness, Sgt. Seibert remained with his platoon and led his men with the highest courage and leadership under heavy shell and machinegun fire. With 2 other soldiers he charged a machinegun emplacement in advance of their company, he himself killing one of the enemy with a shotgun and capturing 2 others. In this encounter he was wounded, but he nevertheless continued in action, and when a withdrawal was ordered he returned with the last unit, assisting a wounded comrade. Later in the evening he volunteered and carried in wounded until he fainted from exhaustion. (US Army n.d.)

In an article entitled "Why Not Shotguns for the Army?" Milton F. Perry mentions one of the more creative uses of shotguns during World War I:

> With the utmost secrecy, trap shooters were recruited, trained in a hush-hush program, and rushed overseas. At Chateaux-Thierry [sic] modern shotguns fired with world-wide reverberations, though the public did not know it until afterwards. A German attack was imminent; and it was *the* drive of 1918. Americans were rushed to bolster the line: marines, infantry and shotgunners.
>
> In outposts ahead of the main line of resistance we placed some of our very best trapshooters – men who could hit a flying bird upon instantaneous reflex action. In the trenches was a unit composed of those who had shot at sporting meets back home. Breathlessly they awaited the assault.

Defending a trench (opposite)

In the Somme sector in April 1918, members of the US 165th Infantry Regiment face a raid by German storm troopers, who quite likely expect the newly arrived Americans to be easy prey. One German is armed with a 9×19mm P 08 pistol with snail drum magazine holding 32 rounds; storm troopers sometimes used this higher-capacity magazine with the LP 08 Artillery Luger but also used it with the standard P 08 as well. The other German wields the 9×19mm Bergmann MP 18/I submachine gun, which also took the snail drum. The US soldier on the right is engaging the raiders with his Colt M1911 pistol. He also has his trench knife at the ready in his left hand. The US soldier at the left, braced against the trench wall, has just snap-fired his Winchester M97 Trench Gun from an unorthodox position, and is lucky not to have bruised or even dislocated his right arm. He carries a holstered Colt M1911 pistol and over his left shoulder he has the pouch for carrying 32 shotgun shells. This early in the US involvement, the shells would still have been paper, which did not hold up well in trench-warfare conditions.

Their first warnings were German "potato masher" hand grenades lobbing through the air. Few landed as most of them were exploded in the air by the experts in the outposts. Upon the failure of the grenade attack, the enemy launched a mortar attack. Again the trapshooters proved their worth, deflecting the slowly arching bombs. Finally, a vast grey [sic] wave of the Kaiser's best surged forward. (Perry 1956: 33)

Although the author has seen mentions of US troops using shotguns to deflect grenades, this is the first reference he has seen to an organized effort to deploy shotguns to stop grenades and even mortar rounds. Certainly, it would make some sense to deploy skilled trapshooters for this purpose, but if the account is true it appears unlikely that this became a common tactical use of the shotgun! It should be borne in mind, too, that many grenades would have been thrown at night by German trench raiders when it would have been virtually impossible to use the grenades as targets.

In an attempt to test this tactic, Jenkins mentions that he had examined dummy Mills bombs used for "counter grenade" training and obtained some of them which were taken to a skeet range and shot at with an M97 Trench Gun with bayonet mounted and using 00 buckshot:

We found the bombs could not only be hit, but we shattered one of those cast-iron dummies in the air, with buckshot? Yet let me rise to remark that, while it is alright to stand and shoot at the incomers at skeet stations 1 and 7 – IF the said incomer were an iron bomb weighing 27 ounces and timed to explode in 5 seconds from its start, and you had 20-inch cylinder-bore shotgun with 9 pellets of shot with which to hit it and knock it away – *what would you do?* I cannot escape a strong conviction that all world's sprint records would be broken in the next instant of time by somebody moving, so to speak, away from there! (Jenkins 1935: 22)

Jenkins also states that using an M97 Trench Gun and skeet loads they fired at skeet targets to check the balance and handling of the shotgun. They hit 17 of 25 targets thrown.

In fact, some years ago the author and a friend discussed the likelihood of shooting grenades out of the air as they were thrown after reading an account of this during World War I. After obtaining a dummy "potato masher" grenade intended for use by reenactors, they took turns throwing the grenade from behind a berm while the other attempted to knock it out of the air with a trench shotgun. In a total of 20–25 throws, only once did the pattern of shot hit the grenade and deflect it. Neither the author nor his friend had much experience shooting trap and skeet, it should be noted.

Perry discusses the effect of the shotgun against German attackers during the same engagement. The "anti-grenade" gunners retreated to the American lines. Joining other shotgun-armed Americans, they held fire until the Germans were within 50yd, then sent a withering hail of 00 buckshot as they repeatedly pumped their trench guns. The German assault was broken, and the Germans retreated (Perry 1956: 33). Perry speculates that at close range, the shotgun was even more effective than the machine gun:

Back in the training camps we had discovered that every buckshot round spewed over an area some nine feet high and three feet wide, and perforated a two-inch board at 100 yards. Even at 150 yards at least one slug usually hit a man-sized target. What was even more important was that a shotgunner, firing from the hip, with a loader beside him could get off as many as fifty shots a minute – by simply twitching the trigger and pumping. (Perry 1956: 33)

This advertisement for DuPont portrays the M97 Trench Gun and makes reference to its alleged use to shoot grenades out of the air. (Author)

The author has substantial experience using pump-action fighting shotguns and finds the comments about the shotgunner firing from the hip while a loader inserts shells into the shotgun rather optimistic. The bottom-loading M97 does allow relatively fast reloads by the operator, but for a loader to attempt to insert shells while the shooter is firing, dealing with recoil, and operating the pump action would be very difficult, especially if the shooter were firing from the hip, as the loader would have to be kneeling! Perhaps the "loader" was actually intended to just hand cartridges to the shooter to speed reloading. It is also possible that each team had two shotguns, with one being loaded as the other was fired.

Perry does mention some other uses of the trench gun. In a return to the shotgun's roots as a "fowling piece," American troops supposedly used their trench guns to knock down German carrier pigeons and capture messages. Presumably, some birdshot would have been available to allow a better pattern than 00 buckshot. He also reports that Allied airmen used shotguns to shoot at enemy balloons and aircraft (Perry 1956: 33). Given the fragility of World War I aircraft, shotgun fire could have wreaked havoc with the engine or controls.

Jenkins mentions the report of one infantry captain about the effectiveness of the trench guns:

…his men had one good chance with them [the trench guns] at a German mass attack upon his trench – with nine .34 caliber buckshot per load, 6 loads in the gun, 200-odd men firing, plenty more shells at hand – the front ranks of the assault simply piled up on top of one another in one awful heap of buckshot-drilled men. (Jenkins 1935: 22)

Jenkins continues: "The shotguns went right on at their business – so terrible a success that message after message from G.H.Q. to America begged: 'Give us more shotguns!' and by November 1918 two more models (Winchester hammerless and Remington) were about to be brought into production; when the Germans cried 'Enough!'" (Jenkins 1935: 22)

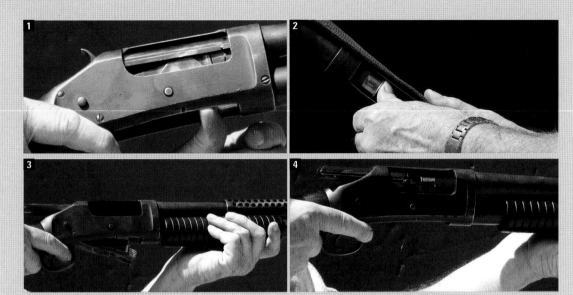

Loading and firing the M97 Trench Gun

The tubular magazine was loaded by thrusting shells into it through the bottom loading port (**1** & **2**). Marines and doughboys found that normally the most efficient method for loading it was to turn the M97 to the side while pushing the shells into the magazine with enough force that they were fully seated.

To chamber a round, the forearm had to be thrust forward to release the bolt lock, or if the hammer was down the bolt was automatically released and the action could be operated. There is also a small bolt-release button on the left side of the receiver, which could be depressed to allow the action to be cycled.

However, it was quite small and most troops found it faster to just push the forearm forward or decock the hammer. Of course, when a round was fired the bolt release operated automatically since the hammer was down. Because the bolt was exposed, as was the carrier when operating the action, troops learned to keep the M97 Trench Gun clear of their equipment when cycling the action. Note that the carrier has picked up a round and is raising it to enter the chamber as the bolt goes forward (**3**). When chambering a round the forearm was run forward with some force to make sure the round was fully chambered (**4**). The weapon was then ready to fire.

On October 8, 1918, troops of the US 33rd Division were ordered to cross the Meuse River near the village of Brieulles. Their target consisted of German guns located at the Borne de Cornouiller on the Consenvoye Heights. Also taking part in the assault were troops of the US 29th Division. With troops of the 29th in support, members of the 33rd Division crossed the Meuse. One 33rd Division sergeant made good use of his trench gun in attacking German machine-gun positions:

> Here fighting for position and exploiting of the woods at the base of the Cornouiller was distinguished by the same versatility and daring of Doughboy sergeants and officers that was displayed by men of the 29th, both divisions demonstrating various ways of taking machine-gun nests from veterans that had nothing to do with classroom lectures or textbook tactics. One of the 33rd's Medal of Honor performers was First Sergeant Johannes S. Anderson. First Sergeants were armed with the Army's brutal Colt .45 automatic, which left an exit hole in a man's back the size of a derby hat; but the Chicago sergeant, undergoing much hostile fire to reach a concrete pillbox, made his entrance through the stage door of the pestiferous machine-gun nest bearing a

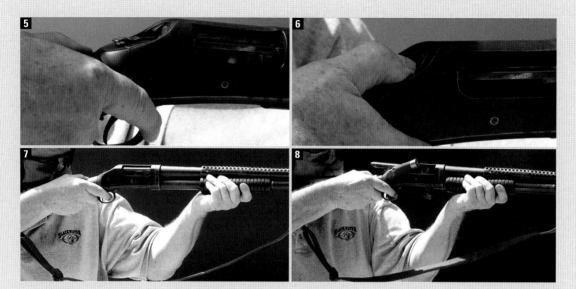

Note that once a round was chambered, the hammer was cocked (**5**). The M97 Trench and Riot Guns did not have a safety. The hammer could be lowered to half cock, but this was not a completely safe method for carrying the M97. Normally, the safest method was to wait to chamber a round until combat was imminent. However, during night raids or other circumstances where sound could reveal his position, the doughboy or Marine would have chambered a round before entering No Man's Land.

One method for increasing safety was to carry the M97 with the thumb between the hammer and firing pin (**6**). This method of blocking the hammer would only have been used when advancing into action with a round in the shotgun's chamber. When going into action with a round chambered, the soldier might also "top off" the magazine by inserting a round to replace the one that had been chambered.

When firing the M97 Trench Gun (**7**), the bead front sight could be used, though at close quarters the shotgun would likely just be aimed at the enemy's torso. The support hand was placed on the handguard in such a way as to offer good support when shooting but also sufficient leverage to operate the slide action. Once a round had been fired, the slide action was operated smartly to be sure it ran fully back, ejecting the spent case and reaching position so that when the forearm was thrust forward a new round was chambered (**8**).

sawed-off shotgun. Two buckshot blasts and the twenty-three performers left on their feet surrendered ... (Stallings 1963: 304)

In his excellent book *Complete Guide to United States Military Combat Shotguns*, Bruce Canfield offers some of the evaluations by officers of the shotgun's effectiveness in combat. Colonel J. B. Bennett of the 11th Infantry, 5th Division, felt that the shotguns performed admirably in trench raiding and patrols in "No Man's Land." Other officers comment that the shotgun had proven very effective at night and at close range. Some also mention how demoralizing it was to the Germans. The major complaint was that the paper cartridges were not reliable in the damp conditions often encountered in the trenches. Because of these problems, prior to a raid, doughboys often ran every shotgun shell they had through their trench gun to make sure they would feed reliably, with any showing a problem being discarded. Also, since the shotguns were loaded and unloaded frequently, the paper cartridge cases would deform, making them unreliable. Some officers also commented that the shotgun was not effective in their sectors, which entailed fighting in open country, but then this was not the combat shotgun's forte. There were also some complaints about the lack of a good belt or pouch for carrying shotgun shells (Canfield 2007: 36). Two of these complaints were addressed in 1918. Shotgun shells using brass cases were ordered but only a limited number of them made it to France prior to the end of hostilities. To allow shotgun shells to be carried more effectively (and protected from the mud of the trenches), a 32-round canvas pouch was developed, but few made it to France. For the most part, infantrymen just carried the shotgun shells in their pockets.

According to Canfield, shotguns were issued to the US 5th, 26th, 32nd, 35th, 42nd, 77th, and 82nd Divisions (Canfield 2000: 135). Although a limited number of Remington M10 Trench and Riot Guns as well as some M97 Riot Guns were acquired by the War Department for service in France, it was generally the M97 Trench Gun that saw combat.

BETWEEN THE WORLD WARS

After World War I, the shotgun continued to be used by US troops. Labor unrest following the war resulted in shotguns being kept in various arsenals around the United States for issuance to troops assigned to quell rioting workers. As a result of a series of mail robberies between 1919 and 1921 in which $6,000,000 was taken, in 1921 the US Post Office requested that US Marines be assigned as mail guards. As a result, on November 7, 1921 President Harding sent the following letter to Secretary of the Navy Edwin Denby:

During the 1920s US Marines were assigned to guard the US Mail after a series of robberies. These Marines guarding a mail car are armed with M97 Trench Guns. (NARA)

My Dear Mr. Secretary:

You will detail as guards for the United States Mails a sufficient number of officers and men of the United States Marine Corps to protect the mails from depredations by robbers and bandits.

You will confer with the Postmaster General as to the details, and will issue the necessary instructions in regard to the performance of this duty.

Very truly yours,
Warren G. Harding (Quoted in Corney 1993)

Fifty-three officers and 2,200 enlisted Marines were assigned as mail guards, armed with Colt M1911 pistols, Smith & Wesson and Colt M1917 revolvers, M1903 rifles, and trench shotguns (Winchester M97s and Remington M10s). Denby, himself a former Marine, issued tough orders to the Marines:

You must, when on guard duty, keep your weapons in hand and, if attacked, shoot and shoot to kill. There is no compromise in this battle with bandits. If two Marines guarding a mail car, for example, are suddenly covered by a robber, neither must hold up his hands, but both must begin shooting at once. One may be killed, but the other will get the robbers and save the mail. When our Marine Corps men go as guards over the mail, that mail must be delivered or there must be a dead Marine at the post of duty. (Quoted in Corney 1993)

Marines armed with M97 Trench Guns and M1911 pistols guard the US Mail during the 1920s. (NARA)

The reputation of the Marines was such that once they assumed their duties as mail guards, the robberies ceased, not one being committed before the Marine guards were withdrawn on March 15, 1922. However, in March 1923 a mail messenger was robbed of $2,400,000 in registered mail. Then in October 1923 a robber shot a mail-truck driver during another robbery. Once again, a total of 2,500 Marines were assigned as mail guards. By 1926, robbers were armed with Browning Automatic Rifles (BARs) and submachine guns (SMGs), so the Marines added Thompson SMGs to their pistols and shotguns for mail-guard duty. In February 1927, many of the Marines assigned to mail-guard duty were needed for deployment to Nicaragua and were relieved by newly trained postal-security agents.

Although some of the shotguns used for mail guard duty were returned to the Ordnance Department by the Post Office, those that were drawn from Marine armories stayed with the Marines and went to Nicaragua, where reportedly they performed well on counterinsurgency operations, though the shortage of brass cartridges was once again a problem in the moist, humid climate. Marines from the 4th Marines were also assigned as guards on Yangtze Rapid Steamship Company boats traveling on the Yangtze River between 1933 and 1935. Although their favored weapon was the BAR, some trench shotguns were also used to repel river pirates. Canfield lists the shotguns on hand with the USMC Legation Detachment in Peking on July 1, 1939 as five Remington M10s, 11 Winchester M97s, and six Winchester M12 Riot Guns (Canfield 2007: 72). Note that in inventory documents "trench guns" were often designated as "riot guns," so some of these were likely trench guns.

During the late 1930s, the Ordnance Department considered converting some of the riot guns on hand to trench gun configuration. Some of these "riot" guns were actually World War I-era trench guns, the ventilated handguards of which had been damaged and discarded. An inventory of July 1, 1940 showed a total of 21,187 military shotguns in US Government inventory, the bulk of which were Winchester M97s. As the Ordnance Department considered possible shotgun procurement, on August 7, 1941, four types of shotguns (in addition to the M97 already in wide use) were standardized for military procurement: Winchester M12, Ithaca M37, Remington M31, and Stevens M620A (Canfield 2007: 75).

October 10, 1944: Marines supervise "water call" at the Japanese prison stockade of the 1st Marine Division. Though not stated, this photograph was probably taken on Peleliu. The Marine in the center is armed with a shotgun. (NARA)

WORLD WAR II

After the Pearl Harbor attack, the need for combat shotguns became even more acute. Every M1 Garand rifle, M1903 rifle, and M1 carbine would be needed for combat troops. Hence, troops assigned to guard duties in the USA, MPs, and others could be armed with shotguns. On February 25, 1942, the Adjutant General of the Army, Major General Emory S. Adams, requested a survey from each Army Corps area of the numbers of rifles and .45 pistols which could be replaced with shotguns (Canfield 2007: 78). Not only were shotguns ordered from arms manufacturers, but in the immediate aftermath of Pearl Harbor representatives of various Ordnance depots purchased some shotguns directly from local sporting good stores. Although the US armed forces had traditionally used only 12-gauge combat shotguns, some 16-gauge shotguns were acquired in the early days of World War II to arm Coast Guard personnel responsible for patrolling US beaches to prevent enemy saboteurs or spies from landing. Making the need for shotguns even greater was their use to train aerial gunners and naval antiaircraft gunners.

The need for shotguns for combat units was filled from stocks on hand and new production. To speed acquisition of military shotguns, many manufacturers produced military riot guns using receivers on hand, often with engraved game scenes. Military Remington M11 semiautomatic riot guns are often encountered with commercial features. Checkered wood is also often encountered on various early-production military shotguns as those stocks and forearms on hand were used up.

Wartime use of the shotgun varied substantially between the European and Pacific theaters. In Europe and North Africa, the shotgun was used primarily behind the lines by MPs and guards assigned to supply depots or POW compounds. In the Pacific, however, especially among the Marines, the close-quarters fighting in the jungle made the shotgun an appealing weapon.

A memorandum of October 5, 1942 from the headquarters of the 2nd Marine Division sets forth the number of 12-gauge shotguns recommended for different elements of the division as follows: Division Special Troops – 150, Division Service Troops – 50, 6th Marines – 190, 10th Marines – 50, 18th Marines – 50. No explanation is given for the much larger number required by the 6th Marines, although the regiment landed on Guadalcanal on January 4, 1943. In most cases 200 cartridges per shotgun were allotted, although the 6th Marines were allotted 205 rounds per shotgun and the 10th Marines 320 rounds per shotgun (Canfield 2007: 98).

During World War II the Ordnance Department also acquired Winchester M97 Riot Guns; note the "U.S." markings and Ordnance bomb marking on this M97 Riot Gun. (Courtesy of Rock Island Auction Company)

Stevens M520-30 Trench Guns like this one were used during World War II and up until Vietnam. (Courtesy of Rock Island Auction Company)

On April 1, 1945, US Marines hit Blue Beach No 2 on Okinawa; the Marine in the center foreground is armed with a Winchester M12 Trench Gun. (USMC)

As the war in the Pacific progressed, Marines learned that in a firefight against Japanese *banzai* charges, shotgun ammo was used very quickly. As a result, the number of cartridges per shotgun would be increased again and again. In fact, Canfield mentions that during the fighting on Iwo Jima Marines had to stop using their shotguns and switch to rifles because of a shortage of ammunition (Canfield 2007: 102).

Among the Marine units that used the shotgun to good effect were the Marine Raiders Battalions. As early as the Makin Island Raid on August 17–18, 1942, which was carried out to gather intelligence on the Gilbert Islands and to divert Japanese attention from the landings on Guadalcanal and Tulaga, members of the 2nd Marine Raiders Battalion used their shotguns to deadly effect. The 2nd Marine Raiders Battalion used fire teams with more firepower than a typical Marine one. Normally, in each fire team there were three BARs, three Thompson SMGs, and four M1 Garands. The Raiders managed to get Garands ahead of other Marine units, to a large extent because James Roosevelt, the President's son, was an officer in the battalion. Some Marine Raiders, however, still favored the shotgun. A group of Raiders under Lieutenant "Frenchy" Le Francois had prepared an ambush for one group of Japanese defenders:

The sun at his back worked in Le Francois's favor. It glared in the eyes of the enemy and conveniently outlined Kanemitsu's men. As the Japanese drew closer, Thomason strutted along his line, encouraging the men and reminding them to hold their fire until directed. "Thomason chuckled with glee and patted his shotgun" Le Francois later recalled of his robust sergeant.

Thomason reminded his men to hold their fire until the enemy drew within twenty yards. Suddenly, as Raiders clenched their weapons and squirmed slightly in their positions, Thomason bellowed, "Let 'em have it" and emptied his twelve-gauge shotgun. (Wukovits 2009: 111)

Sergeant Clyde Thomason was a former China Marine who had reenlisted when World War II began. During the Makin fighting he would win a posthumous Congressional Medal of Honor for leading an assault on a Japanese position.

One lesson learned by the Marines on Makin was that though shotguns were effective at killing Japanese, especially when they were charging, they also consumed a large amount of ammunition. In fact, some of the Raiders had to use captured Japanese weapons when their shotguns ran out of ammunition. This, and early encounters in which shotgun ammunition ran low, made the Marines obsessive about having enough ammunition for their shotguns.

During what is generally known as "The Long Patrol" by Carlson's Raiders – the 2nd Marine Raiders Battalion – on Guadalcanal between November 6 and December 4, 1942, Marine Raiders attacked Japanese troops attempting to escape an encirclement in the Koli Point area. During the patrol, Raiders also destroyed Japanese artillery pieces which had been firing on Marine positions, and set ambushes along infiltration routes. During the patrol, the Raiders killed nearly 500 Japanese troops while losing only 16 Raiders.

In writing about his experiences with the Raiders on The Long Patrol, Ervin Kaplan describes the 12-gauge shotgun assigned to a radio unit:

The function of the Raiders was spearheading amphibious landings upon enemy held beaches, raiding enemy installations and raiding and reconnaissance behind enemy lines. The communication section consisted of a radio and a telephone group, which functioned at company and battalion level. These functions demanded light dependable radio equipment, which was asking a great deal of the relatively primitive pre transistor state of radio communication devices at that time. The radio equipment carried ashore at the Aola Bay landing was the "TBX" which consisted of four canvas encased units furnished with pack straps; a transceiver set, a receiver battery box each weighing about forty pounds; in addition, there was a hand cranked generator for transmission weighing in at about twenty five pounds and a 10 pound antennae in sections. The four company radio men were trained in combat techniques as well as in communication. In addition to side arms the radio station was armed with a twelve gauge shotgun firing pea size "00" buckshot. At close range it would blow a four inch diameter hole in a man. (Kaplan n.d.)

The Marines had found that shotguns were very useful in defending static positions such as radio posts or machine-gun positions; hence, it makes sense that a shotgun would be included with the radio equipment. Later in his description of The Long Patrol, Kaplan mentions the shotgun once again:

> The day following our food gathering patrol with four companies out on patrol from Binu, we radio men were kept busy communicating between companies by TBX radios. The radio consisted as previously stated of four units in canvas carrying cases, a transceiver unit, a battery power supply unit, a hand cranked generator and an antennae unit, for protection a twelve gauge shotgun and for ammunition, double aught [00] buckshot. The radio gear was fortunately carried by four very cooperative Solomon Islanders. Our communication team could set up and be operative in thirty seconds. Consequently we could hike with a light load. My pack was a gas mask case which held my food, matches, a good supply of dry socks and a bottle of tincture of merthiolate. We received the message that C Company had been ambushed by a group of escaping Japanese. (Kaplan n.d.)

Among other Marine units known to be especially fond of the shotgun was Major Lewis Burwell "Chesty" Puller's 1st Battalion, 7th Marines on Guadalcanal. On the night of October 24–25, 1942, during the defense of Henderson Field, Marines of Puller's 1/7th held the field against a Japanese attack that lasted three hours and resulted in 70 Marine casualties and 1,400 Japanese killed in action. Puller, the most decorated Marine in the history of the Corps, won his third Navy Cross for the action, in which the Marines' shotguns accounted for a lot of dead Japanese.

The Marines found the shotguns very useful at night when they might have to take a quick area shot when they heard a sound. They also found the shotguns useful in protecting machine-gun positions, which the Japanese would often target during *banzai* attacks. Shotguns were also used at night to guard command posts. By 1944 each Marine regiment's HQ and Service Company was authorized 100 "riot-type" shotguns for security use or issuance to other regimental components as needed (Archer 1988: 26). Reportedly, the Marines considered the shotguns such effective killers that they managed to acquire by any means possible up to three

Clearing a bunker (previous pages)

During the fighting on Tarawa during November 20–23, 1943, US Marines of the 2nd Marine Division clear Japanese troops from a bunker, using an M2 flamethrower. In the foreground are Marines placed to kill any Japanese attempting to escape the flames. The Marine standing at left uses an M12 Trench Gun, which was deadly in close-range encounters. Marines armed with the shotgun carried as many shells as possible since resupply of shotgun ammunition was sometimes spotty. They also used whatever pouches they could find or alter to carry shells, in this case double belts for M1903 Springfield clips. The other two Marines are armed with M1 Garand rifles with bayonets mounted. During the war in the Pacific the Marines would have shown little mercy to Japanese attempting to escape a bunker.

times the shotguns they were normally allotted for the planned assault on the Japanese home islands.

Colonel Cleland E. Early, USMC (Ret.), gave a good explanation of why he chose a shotgun when serving as a company officer in the 2nd Marine Raiders Battalion on Guadalcanal:

US Army troops on Bougainville in late 1943 or early 1944; note that the infantryman at the left is armed with a Winchester M97 Trench Gun. (NARA)

> I had studied and experimented with various weapons to be used in restricted areas and for close-in work. These weapons included the 45-caliber pistol, M-1 Carbine, the Thompson submachine gun, the Reising gun, the BAR, and the M1 rifle. Because of its dispersal, striking power, and non-aimed accuracy, I determined that the shotgun was most acceptable, particularly in the jungle and quick-reaction situations. (Quoted in Archer 1988: 23)

Another Marine Raiders officer found his shotgun effective but discovered it had one disadvantage. Major Richard Washburn came ashore on Guadalcanal with the 2nd Marine Raiders Battalion on November 4, 1942. Some days after landing, Washburn was on a patrol when his troops got into a firefight at a village called Asamana on the Metapona River. According to Washburn:

> At the time I was carrying both a .45 pistol and a shotgun, figuring the scatter gun would be great for quick combat. You just don't have to worry much about aiming a shotgun.

Kwajalein, February 5, 1945: MP PFC Frank Reed uses a M97 Trench Gun to guard supplies. (NARA)

But let me tell you, while the shotgun can be great, it can also get you killed. You know the sound of one of those things is a lot different than that of a rifle. I'm not sure most of those Nips [*sic*; derogatory term for Japanese] had ever heard a shotgun before I opened up at the Metapona.

Whatever, they came back at me as if I were a whole patrol. That's when I caught the bullet in my boot. After that I was very careful whenever I used my shotgun. (Quoted in Berry 1982: 125)

Berry attributed the fact that the bullet did not penetrate to his foot to the fact that the Raiders had been supplied with boots constructed of especially thick, tough leather.

Archer quotes another Marine who found the shotgun very effective. Brigadier General Edwin D. Simmons, USMC (Ret.), who became Director of Marine Corps History and Museums, stated:

I had found my M-1 Carbine inadequate in a firefight and traded it for a shotgun. I used the shotgun in one firefight while on reconnaissance, hitting one Japanese as he stepped into a clearing about 20 yards range. I called my shotgun my "one-inch mortar." I had no problems with it except the cardboard shell casings would get damp and swell. (Quoted in Archer 1988: 26)

In some combat situations, the Marines actually found that the short range of the shotgun was an advantage rather than a disadvantage. According to Eric H. Archer, "At times the limited range of the combat shotgun was in fact an advantage. In the drive on Afetna Point, Saipan, shotguns were issued to every other man in Company G, 2nd Battalion, 8th Marines, to reduce the hazard to flanking troops of the 4th Marine Division" (Archer 1988: 23).

Although the Marines primarily used the M97 and M12 Trench Guns – the ability to mount a bayonet appealed to the Marines' love of this edged weapon – according to Swearengen, a substantial number of M11 Riot Guns also saw action in the Pacific, though he does not mention whether with the Marines or Army (Swearengen 1978: 324). Navy "Seabees" (Construction Battalions) and other naval units also reportedly had some of the Remington semiautomatic weapons. At least one Marine officer in the Pacific preferred a personally-owned double-barreled shotgun. Eric H. Archer describes this Marine colonel:

… Perhaps the best-known Marine to use a shotgun in combat was Colonel William J. Whaling, code-named "Shotgun." When Col. Whaling reported for duty at Headquarters USMC, between two combat tours, an official Marine Corps biographical release advised that Whaling had carried a shotgun when serving with the 1st Marine Division in the Solomons. The Marine Corps writer noted: "It was not uncommon for him to stalk off in the jungle in search of valuable information on the enemy's movements. Eyewitnesses report he carried a double-barrel shotgun. One barrel contained birdshot and the other held buckshot. When he returned, he either had a Jap or some game." (Archer 1988: 21)

June 1944: US Marines search for Japanese in the swamps of Saipan. The Marine at the far right is armed with a Winchester M97 Trench Gun. (USMC)

Archer also reports that members of the 1st Battalion, 7th Marines on Peleliu used shotguns loaded with birdshot to "interdict" Japanese carrier pigeons. He also mentions Cal Lannert, a member of the 5th Marines Scout Sniper Platoon, who normally carried an M12 Trench Gun, which he used on pig hunts when not in combat (Archer 1988: 21).

During 1969, a member of the US Army's 129th MP Company with his Winchester M12 Trench Gun covers a VC suspect picked up during a river patrol along Qui Nhon Bay, Vietnam. (NARA)

KOREA AND VIETNAM

Swearengen offers a good explanation of why the shotgun was not used more widely during the Korean War:

> Korean terrain is open, without appreciable foliage. Most of the timber and brush had long since been consumed to ward off the arctic cold during Siberian-type winters. Such open terrain offered good fields of fire over long ranges for standard infantry weapons. In such terrain shotguns were at a disadvantage. For this reason, they were normally assigned command post defense missions. They were sometimes put on front lines to help cope with Chinese Communist human wave assault tactics. But over the ranges involved, the machine gun was a more suitable weapon for this purpose. When the Chinese did break through the lines, shotguns were unsurpassed in cleaning out the assault squads and restoring the perimeters. (Swearengen 1978: 215)

Because of the problems with pilfering at US supply depots, shotguns were widely used by guards, at least partially for their deterrent effect as well as their close-combat effectiveness. Jack Walentine, who served with the 25th Infantry Division in Korea, recounts the situation in which he found the venerable M97 Trench Gun useful:

At one point I got a hold of a Model 97 shotgun from the MP company and had it for a while. If I was on a listening post at night, I'd carry that shotgun. On a listening post your average shot was maybe eight to ten feet. I used that shotgun several times; it was an excellent piece of equipment. (Goodwin 2006: 90)

April 30, 1967: on Hill 881 near Khe Sanh, Vietnam, Sergeant R. E. Ferdeit, a member of the 3rd Marines, is on the lookout for VC with his Winchester M12 Trench Gun. (USMC)

On listening posts, which would be positioned ahead of US lines, the ability to eliminate multiple attackers quickly, especially at night, would have made the shotgun highly effective.

The Vietnam War proved much more conducive to the use of the combat shotgun than Korea. As in the Pacific during World War II, the jungle fighting in Vietnam allowed the deadly effect of the shotgun at close range to be maximized. Most US infantry units had at least a few shotguns available to arm the point man on patrols or when assigned perimeter guard duty. In some cases, dog handlers used shotguns to clear by fire an area to which their dogs had alerted. Shotguns were also used by MPs to guard captured Viet Cong or to provide security for installations. When guarding ammunition dumps, fuel depots, and other installations where rifle ammunition could cause explosions or damage expensive equipment, shotguns were often chosen to arm the guards.

A substantial number of combat shotguns were supplied to the South Vietnamese government with the intent that they would be used by village-defense militias, but unless issued directly by US Special Forces advisors most did not make it into the hands of the villagers. At least a few of these shotguns were also used by US Special Forces members. Ithaca M37 Riot Guns were supplied to the ARVN and, once again, a few probably saw use with US advisors. A substantial number of

April 1, 1966: US Army MPs guard the recently bombed Victoria Hotel in Saigon. The MP in the center is armed with a Stevens M77E Riot Gun. (NARA)

Remington M870 Riot Guns were supplied to the ARVN as well. Reportedly, at least some Winchester M12 Trench Guns were built before or just after Winchester stopped producing the M12 in 1964 and sent for use by the Vietnamese.

US troops continued to use Winchester M97 and M12 Trench Guns and Stevens M520-30 Trench Guns left in the inventory in Vietnam. Among the new shotguns acquired for use in Vietnam was the Ithaca M37 Riot Gun and a small number of Ithaca trench guns. The US Navy SEALs made extensive use of the M37 shotgun on ambushes and raids. In some cases, these shotguns were fitted with the "duck-bill" shot diverter/spreader. SEAL Chief James Watson made substantial use of combat shotguns in Vietnam and describes his experiences in *Point Man*. During his first tour in Vietnam during 1967, Chief Watson comments on weapons the SEALs were using, including shotguns:

Before we left Can Tho, a bunch of new and deadly toys had come in from the States. Our first Stoner machine gun had arrived, along with the instructions and a supply of extra ammunition and the links. Since there was only one Stoner for Second Platoon at the time, we had left it back with the other squad. But other items had come in that we took with us. Bob Gallagher now had a Remington 7188, a selective-fire 12-gauge shotgun. With the selector switch set to full automatic, the 7188 would empty its eight-round magazine in about one second. Quite a handful of firepower …

The devils with green faces (previous pages)

Some time in 1969, US Navy SEALs launch an ambush along a Viet Cong infiltration route in the Mekong Delta. The "Devils with Green Faces," as the VC sometimes termed the SEALs, were famous for decimating the VC with ambushes such as the one illustrated. In this case the SEALs have set a parallel ambush (all firing from the same side parallel to the enemy). They have waited until the boat with the largest number of enemy fighters is in the kill zone to open up with devastating firepower. The SEAL at left fires the Stoner M63 light machine gun favored by the SEALs. While his colleagues eliminate the enemy in the lead boat he turns his weapon on the second boat. The SEAL kneeling in the foreground is firing an Ithaca M37 shotgun with the duck-bill spreader choke used by the SEALs. The third SEAL, in the water, fires the Heckler & Koch G3 rifle favored by the SEALs in Vietnam. The SEALs had quite a bit of leeway in weapons and uniforms. As seen here, though, Tiger Stripes and denim jeans were often worn. In many cases, the SEALs operated barefoot.

... Bob Gallagher set up a target range for us to try out all the new weapons. To be sure that none of the VC could see our new hardware we only used the range at night. Bob liked the shotgun, even though it was a bitch to hang on to during full automatic fire ... (Watson & Dockery 1993: 180)

Although Bob Gallagher had been impressed with the fast-firing Remington M7188 initially, that impression didn't last after using it in combat for a while:

... Other weapons were in the gun shed, including the Remington 7188 full-auto shotgun. When the weapon had first arrived, Bob had grabbed onto it as the best thing since sliced bread ... I had started carrying a shotgun, a five-shot Ithaca Model 37. Bob tried to convince me that the Remington 7188 was the weapon for a point man to carry. But I considered it just too heavy. Besides, my pump-action repeater was much more reliable than that complicated full-auto weapon.

Bob carried the 7188 on about six patrols and finally gave up on it as just being too sensitive to dirt. The fact that I could take my Ithaca and just rinse it off in a muddy stream was one of the reasons I liked it. During one ambush, Bob used the 7188 on full auto, and the results were devastating. But the reliability problem finally caused Bob to switch to another Ithaca like mine or the CAR-15 and M-16 rifle.

My favorite shotgun ammunition was the XM-257 round with the hardened lead #4 buckshot. The twenty-seven pellets in the shell would knock down any VC I aimed at, which was exactly what I wanted. The flechette shells that were sent to us later would certainly kill a man, at even longer ranges than the XM-257. But the sharp-pointed little flechettes – they looked like finishing nails with fins – wouldn't stop a man as quickly as a load of #4 buckshot. (Watson & Dockery 1993: 188–89)

During the Vietnam era, Ithaca M37 Riot Guns and a few M37 Trench Guns were acquired for US military usage. The M37 shown here has one of the types of "duck-bill" chokes sometimes seen on the M37, especially in use with the US Navy SEALs. (Jeff Moeller & Mike Spradlin)

BELOW LEFT Close-up of the "duck-bill" spreader choke of the type used by US Navy SEALs on Ithaca M37 shotguns in Vietnam. (Jeff Moeller & Mike Spradlin)

BELOW RIGHT Variation of the "duck-bill" choke used on Ithaca M37 shotguns in Vietnam. (Jeff Moeller & Mike Spradlin)

In addition to reliability problems, the SEALs also found that the full-automatic M7188 went through ammunition too quickly.

Chief Watson relates one incident that illustrates his Ithaca's stopping power on an enemy: "Motioning to Ronnie to cover me, I signaled that I was going to move up. Placing my 12-gauge in the crook of my arm, I signaled for Gallagher to move up the far side of the hooch... My shotgun had five rounds in it, and I had an additional fifty rounds loose in my pockets" (Watson & Dockery 1993: 192). A VC exited the hooch and Watson covered him with his shotgun; however, the VC reached for a weapon:

> The business end of a 12-gauge must look like a five-inch cannon when you're looking at it from the wrong side. I thought for sure that I had my man under control and he would do what I wanted. I was wrong.
>
> Moving so fast that I couldn't really tell how he did it, the man in front of me bent forward, hunched his shoulders, and now had an AK-47 in his hands. As he swung the gun up toward me and fired his first shot, I let go with the shotgun ...
>
> My first load of #4 buckshot smashed into the man's chest and flipped him over backward. *Clack-chunk* – I racked another round into the shotgun and moved forward. He was still moving! *Blam! Clack-chunk ... blam! Clack-chunk ... blam!* I was running toward the hut, shooting as I went.
>
> As I fired my fourth round, my left hand went into my pocket and started feeding rounds into my weapon. Men started pouring from all sides of the hut. Working the action without conscious thought, I ripped off another five rounds from my shotgun. (Watson & Dockery 1993: 192–93)

As does any well-trained user of a combat shotgun, Watson made it a point to reload the tubular magazine whenever he had a chance. The location of the loading port on the bottom of the shotgun would have speeded up the loading process.

In addition to the Ithaca M37 Riot Guns, Stevens M77E Riot Guns were also used by US troops in Vietnam. Reportedly, the stock had a tendency to break off under hard usage such as buttstroking or otherwise striking an enemy.

On Operation *Ivory Coast*, the Son Tay Raid into North Vietnam to rescue US POWs, the raiders did not carry standard US military pump-action shotguns, but instead acquired "a substitute five-shot automatic 12-gauge duck-bill shotgun from a sporting goods catalog," which proved to be more efficient and deadlier (Gargus 2007: 28). No further information is given about the specific make of the shotguns. It may be presumed that the shotguns were intended for use in the actual cellblocks where POWs were held, to eliminate NVA guards quickly without worry about bullets over-penetrating and hitting prisoners.

BEYOND VIETNAM

Although the Remington M870 Mk I shotguns were developed for the US Marines during the Vietnam era, few, if any, actually saw combat in Vietnam. Reportedly, the first significant combat use of the M870 Mk I was during the May 15, 1975 assault to recapture the US container ship SS *Mayaguez*, which had been seized by the Khmer Rouge. During this operation, many sources state the US Marines carrying out the rescue operation used M870 Mk I shotguns. The author has read after-action reports and searched other references to use of the shotguns, but has not found any, though photos of troops carrying what appear to be M870s during the boarding exist. Shotguns are well suited to ship assault and would have been a likely choice. Although the *Mayaguez* operation was considered a success as the ship and crew were freed, the US suffered 59 casualties and lost three helicopters on the mission. Other Remington M870 Riot Guns did see combat in Vietnam with the US Navy and USMC.

In the years after the Vietnam War, the shotguns in armories served MPs and other units for security duties around bases, at embassies, and on board ships. Although at least some M12 Trench Guns and even M97 Trench Guns remained, the primary shotguns in use were the Winchester M1200 and the Remington M870. During Operation *Desert Storm* in January–February 1991, the response to Iraq's invasion of Kuwait, these two shotguns remained the primary models deployed with US troops, though at least some of the recently adopted Mossberg M590 shotguns saw action as well. The primary use of the shotguns seems to have been to protect US positions and supply depots, and to guard Iraqi prisoners. However, it is likely that at least some shotguns saw combat usage during the ground fighting. A traditional use would be in clearing buildings, but in most cases buildings occupied by Iraqi forces were just blasted into rubble!

Bruce Canfield also mentions the use of Winchester M1200 Trench Guns by US Army Rangers during the October 3–4, 1993 battle of Mogadishu (Canfield 2007: 199). Given the close combat within the warrens of Mogadishu, the shotgun would have been a good choice for the Rangers.

A US Marine demonstrates the ready position with the Remington M870 Mk I. (USMC)

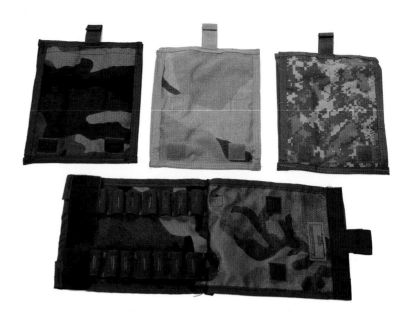

Afghanistan and Iraq

When operations as part of the War on Terror began in Afghanistan and Iraq, the principal shotguns in use with the US armed forces were the Mossberg M500, M590, and M590A1. (The M590A1 features an aluminum trigger guard and safety as opposed to plastic and a heavier barrel, the latter per US Navy specifications.) The USMC standard shotgun as of November 2001 was the Benelli M1014, though Remington M870 and Mossberg M590A1 shotguns remained in use for some time. Some US Army units have also used the M1014. Because of the large number of building entries carried out in Iraq and, to some extent, Afghanistan, some Mossbergs set up as breaching weapons with pistol grips and special stand-off breaching barrels have been used to blow off locks and hinges. Note that in addition to doors, the breaching shotguns have seen substantial use in breaching gates.

Troops using the Mossbergs and the M1014 have noted certain advantages of each. The tang-mounted safety of the Mossberg allows very fast operation while bringing the shotgun to the shoulder to fire. Those using the M1014 like its collapsible stock as this makes it easier to stow the weapon in HUMMVEEs (High Mobility Multipurpose Wheeled Vehicles) or more comfortable when using body armor, since the length of pull (distance between the front of the trigger and the center rear of the butt plate) can be adjusted. The rail atop the M1014 is another good feature, as it readily allows the mounting of night-vision sights, illuminators, etc. Of course, the ability to fire the M1014 without having to move the support arm, as with the pump-action shotgun, allows it to be fired more readily prone or using other types of cover – and very fast.

In his article on the use of the shotgun in the Brigade Combat Team, First Sergeant (Ret.) D. Robert Clements offers a good summation of the doctrine for employment of the combat shotgun during the War on Terror:

Military shotgun loads: Korea to Afghanistan

Through the Korean War and the early Vietnam years, the M19 rounds procured at the end of World War II remained the standard-issue buckshot loads. As the inventory of M19 brass shells became depleted, the Ordnance Department determined that plastic-cased shot shells were as moisture-resistant as brass-cased ones and adopted the "12 Gauge, Shotgun Plastic Case, No. 00 Buckshot, XM162" round. The shells were made of red plastic, the standard color used for 12-gauge shells to differentiate them from other-gauge shells, and marked "00B" on the case. The "X" was designated experimental and remained in the designation for many years but was eventually dropped, and the M162 has remained the standard US military buckshot load for decades.

RIGHT The Whirlpool flechette round developed for use in Vietnam is seen here along with three different types of flechette. (Author)

Also loaded during the Vietnam War were No 4 buckshot cartridges. These loads had the advantage of more pellets – 27 – than the 00 loads – nine – but the No 4 buckshot also gave less penetration. These loads were designated XM257, eventually becoming standardized as M257. The M257 round has seen some use and remains available, but the M162 load is much more widely used.

Among the more interesting shotgun loads developed for use in Vietnam were the flechette loads. The USMC had originally suggested development of a "Beehive" 12-gauge shotgun load using flechettes sometime during the early 1960s. A limited quantity of 12-gauge flechette rounds were produced and tested by the US Army and USMC during 1967 and 1968. The US Navy SEALs also used some of the flechette loads. Flechette rounds, which fired fin-stabilized darts, had better range than buckshot, but lacked the close-range stopping power. Although some troops liked the flechettes, they were not used after the Vietnam War.

As a result of a 1967 request by the US Navy SEALs, AAI Corporation, which had been involved in the flechette project along with Winchester, Remington, and Whirlpool, developed a "silent" shotgun shell. Loaded with No 4 buckshot, the silent shell used a system in which the cup containing the shot was pushed forward by the propellant to fire the buckshot from the barrel, while the extended cup which stayed in the shell prevented the gases, flash, and virtually all of the noise from escaping. The shell proved to have short range and low penetration. It was also expensive

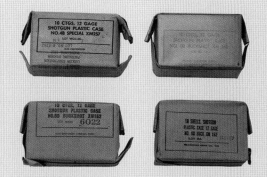

ABOVE Vietnam-era plastic-cased buckshot rounds wrapped ten to a paper packet. The plastic-cased rounds held up well in the jungle environment. (Jeff Moeller & Mike Spradlin)

RIGHT Breaching rounds of the type used to take locks or hinges off doors or gates in Iraq and Afghanistan. (Author)

BELOW LEFT Sectionalized views of two special shotgun rounds used by the US Navy SEALs: at left the "silent" shotgun shell, and at right the flechette round. (Bill Woodin)

to manufacture. Reportedly, only 200 test rounds were delivered to the US Naval Ordnance Testing Laboratory in White Oak, Maryland, before the project was dropped.

Because US troops have had to carry out so many house searches in Iraq in an attempt to capture insurgents, the use of shotguns for door breaching has been extensive. In some cases standard M162 buckshot loads have been used, but shells loaded with solid slugs have also been used to take out hinges or locks. Special frangible* door-breaching rounds of the type developed for use by urban Special Weapons and Tactics (SWAT) teams have also seen substantial use. For military issue, these "12 GA, DOOR BREACHING" rounds are packed in five-round boxes. Also used in Iraq are "less-lethal" rounds designed to disperse crowds. Although acquired primarily to deal with problems at detention facilities, these rounds can also be used to deal with rioters or other crowds. These cartridges are also packed in five-round boxes, which are marked "12 GA. NON-LETHAL CROWD DISPERSAL M1013." These loads appear to be of the rubber buckshot type. Also available is the M1012 load, which is of the rubber rocket type. It is quite likely that USMC Embassy Guards also have both these rounds available.

* Frangible rounds break into fragments, making them less likely to injure the user.

LEFT One of the types of less-lethal ammunition used by US armed forces is the "rubber rocket" shown at middle left, along with other types of less-lethal ammunition. Note that the box shown here is not the type used for US military ammunition. (Author)

The shotgun should be employed in one of two methods. In the first method, the shotgun is employed as a primary weapon with a full stock. Considerations for the commander when employed in this manner are the limited range and reduced ammo capacity of the shotgun. A Soldier conducting house-to-house fighting at close ranges may be well served by the standard shotgun. However, skills that must be ingrained are: reloading constantly or the "load what you shoot" rule and transitioning to a handgun. With only six rounds at their disposal, a shotgunner may find himself out of ammo quickly in a fire fight. Reloads must occur at every lull in the fight. Transitioning to a handgun is one method of staying in the fight if you run out of ammo. Simply put, the shotgun is lowered and the M-9 is drawn, and a controlled pair fired when the shotgun is out of ammo. The shotgunner maintains the M-9 until the situation allows him to reload the shotgun. The same process is used for a stoppage that cannot be cleared by immediate action.

In the second method, the shotgun is employed as a secondary weapon. In this case the primary weapon for the Soldier is the M-4 or M-16. The shotgun is then typically employed with a pistol grip and some sort of retention system. The 10th Mountain's Infantry Mountain Leaders Advanced Marksmanship Course (IMLARM) teaches the shotgun being slung on the firer's side and to transition from the M-4 to the shotgun, then back again.

In the role of a secondary weapon to the M-4, the shotgun is carried uncocked on an empty chamber or with an expended cartridge in the chamber. When employed, the gunner pulls the M-4 across his body away from the shotgun, then brings up the shotgun, racks the slide and fires. Once the engagement is complete, the gunner leaves the shotgun action closed on the expended round and transitions back to the M-4. This process is repeated as required. The gunner will then reload the shotgun when the tactical situation permits. (Clements 2006: 37)

Clements also discusses in his article the need to configure the ammunition carried to expected missions, since 00 buckshot will be choice for offensive operations, breaching rounds for taking down doors during entries, and less-lethal rounds for dispersing crowds. When a soldier carries multiple types of rounds there is always the chance of mixing them up, which could result in situations such as lethal buckshot being fired to disperse a crowd. As a result, troops must have standard procedures for what rounds are carried in their shotguns and for where spare rounds of different types should be carried. Clements advocates that troops should never carry more than two types of shotgun shells at any given time.

Reportedly, US MPs assigned as prison guards in Iraq have Mossberg M500, Winchester M1200, and Remington M870 shotguns available but only loaded with less-lethal rounds. Although current-issue less-lethal shotgun shells use polymer cases that are sturdier than the paper cases used in World Wars I and II, the constant loading and unloading of the shells reportedly has caused damage to them, resulting in cases becoming stuck in the tubular magazine ("Sven556" n.d.).

Captain Ryan Morgan, another veteran of the fighting in Iraq where he served with the 2nd Battalion, 502nd Infantry Regiment, 101st Airborne Division (Air Assault), comments on the use of shotguns. He feels that more shotguns were needed:

> The shotgun proved to be a very useful weapon for my company. We conducted urban operations in five cities during Operation Iraqi Freedom. For all of these missions, the shotgun was the most versatile weapon in our arsenal. The problem was that we only had two in the company. This caused either the squad and platoon to slow down their momentum to bring the shotgun forward, resulting in that Soldier becoming worn out; or conducting breaches by continuous pounding on a lock or a door, a means that did not allow for surprise. The bottom line is that the shotgun should be a squad weapon. Each squad leader should have the option of this weapon in his squad. (Morgan 2004: 13)

Morgan notes that in his unit, the breaching man who carried a shotgun in each squad was armed with the M249 SAW as his primary weapon. The breacher would move to the front of the "stack" and use the shotgun to take the hinges off a door. He would then move aside to let the rest of the team enter as he took up the rear position with his M249. To prevent negligent discharges of the shotgun, the SOP (Standard Operating Procedure) was to have the shotgun's chamber empty except when actually firing a round to take down a door. It was carried with the bolt closed on an empty chamber. When not in use the shotgun would be slung on the user's strong side but away from his primary weapon. An interesting point Morgan makes is that if a breaching muzzle device is not installed on the shotgun to get proper standoff when firing, a metal rod can be attached to the magazine tube to give proper standoff. Note that some standoff distance – an inch or two – is necessary to preclude the likelihood of blowing up the barrel of the shotgun (Morgan 2004: 14).

Although Morgan's unit used the shotgun primarily for breaching, he also found that it was quite effective for crowd control when loaded with less-lethal ammunition. In fact, the intimidation effect of the shotgun was such that a crowd often dispersed just upon hearing the distinctive sound of the pump action being operated and closed. Morgan concludes that: "Throughout Operation Iraqi Freedom's combat, and stability and support operations, the tactical shotgun proved a useful and versatile weapon. It is my belief that the shotgun should become a permanent addition to every infantry squad's arsenal. This change will increase the effectiveness of the infantry squad across the spectrum of missions it is required to perform" (Morgan 2004: 15).

Some new shotguns have been tested for Iraq, notably the select-fire Auto Assault 12 (AA12), which offers a cyclic rate of 300 rounds per minute on full-automatic. It loads from an eight-round magazine or 20- or 32-round drum magazines. The AA-12 was demonstrated to the USMC in 2004. However, to the author's knowledge no contracts have been awarded for the AA12.

The MPS AA12 Assault Shotgun (aka "Sledgehammer") has been tested by the USMC but not yet adopted. (USMC)

Various loop carriers for five shotgun shells currently in use with US troops. (Jeff Moeller & Mike Spradlin)

However, the US Army is now deploying the M26 MASS. Designed to fit under the forearm of an M4 carbine, the 12-gauge M26 uses a straight-pull bolt action and is fed from either a three- or a five-round box magazine. Designed to allow a soldier to have a weapon offering breaching or less-lethal capability along with his M4 carbine without having to carry an additional weapon, the M26 is intended for limited issue. Initially, the Army purchased 1,900 M26 shotguns, then in 2011 a US Army contract for an additional 2,500 M26 shotguns was given to C-MORE Systems, which manufactures the firearm. Early in 2012, the first combat troops to be equipped with the M26 MASS were engineers and MPs of the 2nd Brigade Combat Team, 101st Airborne Division (Air Assault).

Although the mission of the military combat shotgun in Iraq has been more in the breaching and less-lethal role, it still has remained an important part of US Army and USMC armament.

IMPACT
The shotgun's spread

US LAW-ENFORCEMENT USE

In many cases, the influence of shotguns used by the US armed forces might better be termed "cross-pollination" between law-enforcement agencies and the armed forces. For example, before the Winchester M97 Riot Gun was purchased for use by the US Army in the Philippines it had already been successfully used by express messengers, railroad detectives, prison guards, mine guards, and many others. Later, the successful use of the M97 Trench Gun during World War I brought the advantages of the fighting shotgun even more to the attention of civilian security and law-enforcement agencies. Winchester M97 and M12 Riot Guns were widely used throughout the gangster era of the 1920s and 1930s. In fact, Winchester made up at least some M97 Trench Guns for law-enforcement sales during this era. How many of the law-enforcement agencies that purchased them used the bayonet is questionable, though mine or plant guards armed with trench guns mounting bayonets would have been sobering to striking workers.

Although they were still in the USMC, the armed guards assigned to protect the US Mail during the 1920s carried M97 Trench Guns, which proved quite a deterrent to armed robbers. The lesson was not lost on other federal agencies combating heavily armed criminals. Along with the Thompson SMG, Winchester M97 or M12 Riot and Trench Guns became preferred armament for confronting dangerous criminals.

The Ithaca M37 Trench and Riot Guns used in World War II and Vietnam had some influence on the use of that model by law-enforcement agencies. The Los Angeles Police Department (LAPD) was a premier user of the Ithaca M37 Riot Gun for decades. Ithaca also marketed a civilian version of the M37 Trench Gun for use by law-enforcement and security agencies. One of the appeals of the M37 was that, like the Winchester M97 and M12, it was a "slam fire" gun, which allowed quick firing of multiple rounds by holding the trigger back and just operating the slide action. (As a side-note, the current police version of the Ithaca M37 now incorporates a trigger disconnect so that the trigger has to be pulled to fire each round.) In more recent times some US police departments have adopted the Benelli M1014 as well, including the influential LAPD.

FOREIGN USE

The effectiveness of the fighting shotgun in the Pacific during World War II was not lost on the British, who faced a post-World War II counterinsurgency campaign in Malaya. Members of the Special Air Service and other troops made effective close-quarters use of FN Browning semiautomatic 12-gauge shotguns against Communist guerrillas. In at least some cases, special "Malaya loads" were developed by FN, which used buckshot over smaller shot to increase the number of projectiles sent towards the enemy. Other FN loads had zinc cases loaded with nine 00 buckshot pellets. In fact, it was found that in surprise engagements at close quarters, the shotgun was the most effective weapon. Reportedly, too, some users fired their autoloading shotguns tilted to the side so that the recoil would create a swath of projectiles rather than carrying the barrel upward. Some RAF helicopter crewmembers also used Remington M870 or FN Browning A5 shotguns to fire out of the side door at guerrillas spotted from the air (Andrew 2006).

Although no country has embraced the military shotgun to the extent of the United States, the shotgun does see some use with the armed forces of most countries. In many cases, it is used by counterterrorist units, primarily for breaching doors. In Russia, many *Spetsnaz* special-purpose forces units have used an array of shotguns including the 4-gauge KS-23, originally developed to quell prison riots. In addition to buckshot rounds an array of other rounds are available for the KS-23, including a "barricade" round that will reportedly destroy a vehicle's engine block at 100m (109yd). Also available for the KS-23 are less-lethal rounds, stun

The combat shotgun on the big screen

The M97 Riot and Trench Guns have often been used in films portraying the era from just prior to World War I through the 1930s. The use of an M97 usually indicates that the character is a very "serious" individual. Among the author's favorite film portrayals of the M97 were those in *The Professionals* (1966), *The Wild Bunch* (1969), and *The Mummy* (1999). In *The Wild Bunch*, period accuracy dictated that William Holden and Warren Oates carried riot rather than trench models since the action is set prior to the US entry into World War I.

In *The Professionals*, Lee Marvin portrays professional soldier "Rico" Fardan, who carries an M97 Riot Gun, correct since the film is set during the Mexican Revolution. In *The Mummy*, Brendan Fraser as soldier of fortune Rick O'Connell uses his M97 Riot Gun to good effect against vicious reanimated mummies. The distinctive look of the M97 Riot or Trench Gun has made it an especially effective choice to convey that a character is skilled at dealing out death and destruction.

grenades, and tear-gas grenades. Those who have fired the KS-23 state that recoil is quite heavy.

Another notable influence of US military shotguns has resulted from the adoption of the M1014 by the USMC and some other US military units, including the US Navy SEALs. Various other countries have followed the US lead in adopting this combat shotgun, including the United Kingdom, as the L128A1. Some photos showing members of the RAF Regiment training as helicopter snipers for the 2012 London Olympics seemed to show the L128A1 in use with EOTech holographic sights. The use of the combat shotgun for aerial sniping is not necessarily disadvantageous compared to a rifle, as at relatively close range the shotgun pattern is less affected by the movement of the helicopter. Other countries using the M1014 include Australia, Italy, Libya, Ireland, Malaysia, Malta, Slovakia, and Slovenia. In many cases, the M1014 is used by special-forces units. The Irish Army Ranger Wing, for example, which now uses M1014s had previously used Benellis as well in the form of the M3 Tactical model.

April 2010: a member of the USAF's 173rd Security Forces Squadron practices firing from behind cover with his Mossberg M500 shotgun. Note the rifle rear sight forward on the barrel and the Picatinny rail for a red-dot sight. (USAF)

NEW DEVELOPMENTS

The US military use of shotguns has continued to offer impetus to advanced combat-shotgun development. Because of the shotgun's proven value in counterinsurgency warfare, it is likely the US armed forces will continue to evaluate new combat shotguns. This will offer manufacturers the incentive to continue to experiment with advanced combat-shotgun designs.

CAWS

The US military CAWS (Close Assault Weapon System) Program during the early 1980s saw the joint effort of Heckler & Koch and Winchester/Olin to develop a select-fire combat shotgun and the ammunition for it. The weapon was intended to fire multiple projectiles out to 100–150m [109–164yd]. As a result, it would have more range than a typical combat shotgun but less than a combat rifle. As developed the Heckler & Koch CAWS was a bullpup design (with the action set behind the triggergroup) that was only 30in in overall length and used a detachable box magazine. It could be fired as a semiautomatic or on three-round-burst mode.

The ammunition as developed by Winchester/Olin included a load of No 2 buckshot of tungsten alloy with a lead penetrator. This would penetrate .08in of mild-steel plate at 150m (164yd). Also available was a 000 buckshot load, which would penetrate a .75in pine board at 150m. Winchester/Olin was also working on other loads including flechette, fragmentation, incendiary, explosive, and flare. Special SCMITR flechettes, which were more arrow-like and were designed to be aerodynamic and more lethal (by creating a wider wound channel) than previous flechettes, were tested for the CAWS. CAWS ammunition was loaded in a belted brass case, though plastic-cased ammunition was also developed.

The CAWS was not adopted, however, for various reasons including weight (9.5lb) and lack of range compared to the M16/M4 carbine. Although the CAWS offered advantages over the shotguns in use, it was not deemed effective enough to replace an infantry rifle or carbine.

SRM1216

One of the most promising new designs for combat usage is the SRM1216. The SRM1216 is a revolutionary semiautomatic shotgun that overcomes the long-standing problem with military shotguns – magazine capacity. The SRM1216 uses a rotary magazine with four chambers, each holding four rounds, thus giving a capacity of 16 rounds. The magazine, which may be quickly changed, also functions as the forearm for the shotgun. Four rounds may be fired very quickly, at which point the bolt locks back, and the operator rotates the magazine to bring a new chamber into position. At that point, the bolt runs forward chambering a new round, and fire can continue. With practice, the SRM1216 may be operated extremely quickly.

Also available are two shorter versions of the weapon – the SRM1212, which has a shorter barrel and holds 12 rounds, and the SRM1208, which has the shortest barrel and holds eight rounds. Strictly speaking, the SRM1216 is not a bullpup design as the magazine is in front of the trigger, but as with a bullpup, overall length is kept to a minimum. The SRM1216 is 32.5in overall, the SRM1212 27.5in overall, and the SRM1208 24.5in overall.

One of the most innovative of the current generations of military combat shotguns is the SRM1216. (Author)

The author firing the SRM1216, a compact shotgun that fires 16 rounds on semiautomatic very quickly and allows fast reloads with another 16-round forearm/magazine. (Author)

CONCLUSION

The shotgun has remained a widely used military weapon for over a century, and combat in Iraq and Afghanistan has illustrated the continued value of the combat shotgun. Military scatterguns have proven especially useful in jungle insurgencies, where their ability to put a lot of projectiles down-range quickly has enabled them to break ambushes and allow point men to engage the enemy when encountered unexpectedly. Shotguns have also proved to be intimidating weapons for those charged with guarding prisoners or sensitive installations. US Navy ships generally have shotguns in their armories as well, as they still are useful for clearing a deck or repelling boarders. US Embassy Marines also have found shotguns useful for their mission of securing the environs of an embassy from hostile intruders. In urban areas where embassies are normally located, the shotgun grants formidable firepower with less danger of collateral damage to embassy employees or innocent civilians.

One of the most effective uses of the shotgun is as a deterrent. The large muzzle of a 12-gauge shotgun generally does a very good job of causing hostile crowds to disperse or at least back off out of immediate range. However, because the shotgun is a relatively short-range weapon, it is often backed up by troops armed with rifles or carbines to deal with snipers or other threats.

Currently, US troops use the shotgun loaded with less-lethal munitions in both Iraq and Afghanistan to deal with unruly prisoners or hostile crowds. Shotguns may also be used to launch CS-gas projectiles or other chemical munitions to disperse crowds, though US troops would be more likely to use a specialized grenade launcher such as the M203 or M79 to launch gas grenades.

In the urban counterinsurgency campaigns the United States has been involved in as part of the War on Terror, the use of breaching rounds to go through doors or gates has proliferated and become a primary mission of the combat shotgun. In fact, specialized shotguns with stand-off devices at the muzzle and pistol grips are now widely used specifically for breaching.

Because the shotgun has been used for so long and so effectively by US forces, the World War I German arguments that its use does not comply with the Hague Convention have fallen by the wayside. Despite the somewhat misguided notion today that soldiers are social workers in uniform, the mission of the US Army is to destroy those who threaten the security of its country. Through various wars, the United States has found that the shotgun performs that mission well, which is a primary reason it is still an important weapon in US armories.

US Army MPs in China at the end of World War II carry an array of weapons including M1911/M1911A1 pistols, Thompson SMGs, M1 Garand rifle, and the MP seated in the middle has a shotgun. (NARA)

All indications are that the United States will continue to use the Mossberg and Benelli shotguns currently in the armories for the near future. The M26 MASS also seems likely to see at least limited usage. With the expansion of US special-operations forces during the War on Terror, and the emphasis put on their use, it is quite possible that new special-purpose shotguns will be developed for special operators.

From the collector's point of view US military shotguns, especially trench guns, have become more and more sought after. Less than a week before writing this conclusion, the author purchased a Stevens M620A Trench Gun in very fine condition. This is one of the scarcer US trench guns, and the price was almost twice the price he has paid for any other US trench gun in the past. Nevertheless, he was glad to find it.

Trench guns especially conjure up the image of US doughboys or Marines repelling German attacks or assaulting an enemy trench; of US Marines clearing a Japanese bunker or walking point in the jungle; of US Navy SEALs lying in ambush in the Mekong Delta. There is something about picking up a US trench or riot gun and racking the slide that gives the feeling of preparing for dangerous action on the battlefield – a readiness to confront the enemy at close quarters. US military shotguns are not as plentiful on the collector's market as such favorites as the Colt M1911/M1911A1 or the M1 carbine. They are interesting and are getting harder and harder to find. Because it is so utilitarian and deadly the military shotgun is a fascinating weapon, yet one that is less well known than many other US infantry weapons. Hopefully, this book will help acquaint a wider group of readers with the US military shotgun and show why it has been beloved by line infantrymen and special operators likely to face the enemy at close range, as well as by collectors.

BIBLIOGRAPHY

Anonymous (1918a), "Barbarous American Soldiery,"
    Arms and the Man, July 27, 1918: 348

Anonymous (1918b), "Police Train With Riot Guns,"
    Arms and the Man, August 24, 1918: 435

Anonymous (1918c), "Germany, The Shotgun and Reprisal,"
    Arms and the Man, October 12, 1918: 48

Andrew, Martin (2006), "Combat Shotguns in Malaya," *Old War Dogs*
    website, October 21, 2006 – http://www.oldwardogs.
    com/2006/10/combat_shotguns.html, accessed September 7, 2012

Archer, Eric H. (1988), "Military Shotguns of World War II,"
    Gun Digest, 1988 Annual: 20–32

Arnold, James. R. (2011), *The Moro War: How America Battled a
    Muslim Insurgency in the Philippine Jungle, 1902–1913*.
    New York, NY: Bloomsbury Press

Barbour, Bo (2003), "The Evolution of the Army Combat Shotgun,"
    Military Police, April 2003 – http://www.thefreelibrary.com/
    The+evolution+of+the+army+combat+shotgun--
    from+the+blunderbuss+to+the...-a0103384455, accessed
    November 28, 2012

Berry, Henry (1982), *Semper Fi, Mac: Living Memories of the U.S.
    Marines in World War II*. New York, NY: William Morrow

Canfield, Bruce N. (2000), *U.S. Infantry Weapons of the First World
    War*. Lincoln, RI: Andrew Mowbray Publishers, Inc

Canfield, Bruce N. (2007), *Complete Guide to United States Military
    Combat Shotguns*. Woonsocket, RI: Mowbray Publishers, Inc

Clements, Robert (2006), "The Combat Shotgun in the BCT,"
    Infantry Magazine, September–October 2006: 37–41

Corney, George (1993), "Crime and Postal History: Bring in the
    Marines!" *Marine Corps Gazette*, October 1993, 50–52 –
    http://www.mca-marines.org/gazette/crime-and-postal-history-
    bring-marines, accessed September 7, 2012

Gargus, John (2007), *The Son Tay Raid: American POWs in Vietnam
    Were Not Forgotten*. College Station, TX: Texas A&M

Goodwin, Mark G. (2006), *US Infantry Weapons in Combat: Personal
    Experiences from World War II and Korea*. Export, PA:
    Scott A. Duff Publications

Hurley, Vic (2011), *Jungle Patrol: The Story of the Philippine
    Constabulary, 1901–1936*. Salem, OR: Cerberus Books
    (reprint of 1938 edition)

Jenkins, Paul B. (1935), "Trench Shotguns of the A. E. F." *The American
    Rifleman*, November 1935: 14–15, 22

Kaplan, Ervin (n.d.), "A Personal View of The Guadalcanal Long Patrol"
    – http://www.usmarineraiders.org/longpatrolview.htm, accessed
    on September 7, 2012

Leopold, E. A. (1903), "Training Express Guards," *Shooting and Fishing*, February 26, 1903: 412

Long, Samuel Wesley (1918), "The Shotgun Goes to War," TRAPSHOOTING column, *Baseball*, July 1918: 305–07

Morgan, Ryan J. (2004), "The Tactical Shotgun in Urban Operations," *Infantry Magazine*, November–December 2004: 13–15

Olive Drab (n.d.), "Joint Service Combat Shotgun," Olive-Drab website – http://olive-drab.com/od_other_firearms_shotgun_jscs.php>, accessed on November 23, 2012

Parks, W. Hays (1997), "Joint Service Combat Shotgun Program," *The Army Lawyer*, October 1997, 16–24 – http://lawofwar.org/Parks_Combat_Shotguns.htm, accessed September 7, 2012

Perry, Milton F. (1956), "Why Not Shotguns for the Army?" *Guns*, February 1956: 31–33, 58–60

Poyer, Joe (1992), *U.S. Winchester Trench and Riot Guns and other U.S. Combat Shotguns*. Tustin, CA: North Cape Publications

Saunders, Anthony (2012), *Raiding on the Western Front*. Barnsley: Pen & Sword

Stallings, Laurence (1963), *The Doughboys: The Story of the AEF, 1917–1918*. New York, NY: Harper & Row

"Sven556" (2007), "Shotguns in Iraq," Shotgun World.com – http://www.shotgunworld.com/bbs/viewtopic.php?f=7&t=122531, accessed September 7, 2012

Swearengen, Thomas F. (1978), *The World's Fighting Shotguns*. Alexandria, VA: TBN Enterprises

US Army (n.d.), "Medal of Honor Recipients: World War I," US Army Center of Military History – http://www.history.army.mil/html/moh/worldwari.html, accessed September 7, 2012

US Army (1994), *Army Ammunition Data Sheets Small Caliber Ammunition*, FSC 1305. TM 43-0001-27, Headquarters, Department of the Army, April 1994

US Ordnance School (1941), *Shotguns. Ordnance School Text*, OS 9-5. Aberdeen Proving Ground, MD: The Ordnance School, August 1941

US War Department (1942), *Shotguns, All Types*. Technical Manual TM9-285. Washington, DC: War Department, September 21, 1942

Watson, Chief James with Kevin Dockery (1993), *Point Man: Inside the Toughest and Most Deadly Unit in Vietnam by a Founding Member of the Elite Navy SEALs*. New York, NY: William Morrow and Co., Inc

Wukovits, John (2009), American Commando: *Evans Carlson, His WWII Marine Raiders, and America's First Special Forces Mission*. New York, NY: NAL

INDEX